Jon Pearson has practised Aikido fo[...]
presently black belt second Dan. He [...]
Shihan Kitaura and in Californi̤ ͏̤̤ ͏̤̤ ͏̤̤ ͏̤̤ ͏̤̤.
He began teaching Aikido in Spain in 1985 before setting up a
dojo in Bristol in 1987.

Jon Pearson has travelled widely in Europe and North
Africa, and has worked in Israel, Spain and now as a
physiotherapist in America.

AIKIDO

The essential introductory guide

Jon Pearson

Photographs by
Franco Chen
Illustrated by Michael Taylor

V

VERMILION
LONDON

First Published in the United Kingdom in 1991
1 3 5 7 9 10 8 6 4 2

This revised edition published in the united Kingdom in 1997
by Vermilion, an imprint of Ebury Press
   Random House UK Ltd
   Random House
   20 Vauxhall Bridge Road
   London SW1V 2SA

   Random House Australia (Pty) Ltd
   20 Alfred Street, Milsons Point, Sydney
   New South Wales 2016, Australia

   Random House New Zealand Limited
   18 Poland Rd, Glenfield,
   Aukland 10, New Zealand

   Random House South Africa (Pty) Limited
   Box 2263, Rosebank 2121, South Africa

   Random House UK Limited Reg. No. 954009

A CIP catalogue record for this book is available from the
British Library.

ISBN 0 09 1815797

Typeset in Century Schoolbook
Printed and bound in Great Britain by Guernsey Press

Papers used by Vermilion are natural, recyclable products
made from wood grown in sustainable forests.

This book is dedicated to my family, friends and all followers of the Way of *ai-ki*.

CONTENTS

CONTENTS

PREFACE

My intention in writing this book is to feed the minds of would-be Aikido students and beginners with background information, to enable them to see more clearly the path ahead and to be more aware of the significance of their early experiences. I also hope to provide some in-depth analysis and discussion to provoke the interest of the more senior student.

I hope you will be inspired, by what you understand and fail to understand of my writing, to go on to practise Aikido on the mat. I do not aspire to more than that, because only through practice will anyone 'understand' anything. If certain passages are found to be too dense and complex for you at the moment, make a note to return to them at a later date. A certain amount of experience and hindsight may clarify their meaning.

I have given a brief outline of the history of martial arts in Japan and a personal history and philosophy of the Founder of Aikido, this background information being vital to an understanding of Aikido as it exists today. The principles and practice of this form of *budo* are explained in some detail, including how it compares and contrasts with other martial arts. Advanced practice and the use of weapons (specifically *bokken*, a wooden sword, and *jo*, a wooden staff) are given their own chapters; weapons practice is a fundamental part of the origins and current study of Aikido. Finally an insight into the organizational structure in Britain and worldwide is offered.

A bibliography has been included to take the interested student further in his quest for knowledge. There is now a wealth of background texts on the history and philosophy of *budo* in general and Aikido in particular. There are also some excellent texts on Aikido technique. However, I would strongly advise that you do not attempt to learn Aikido without a teacher. Reserve these texts for back-up and background. It cannot be emphasised enough that a textbook, used alone, is not sufficient to learn a martial art safely or correctly.

Practise hard and neither look back nor forward: practise for today.

(The use of the masculine pronoun [he, his etc.] throughout this book reflects the prejudice of the English language and not that of the author. Martial arts are no longer an exclusive male preserve and all statements refer equally to men and women unless otherwise specified.)

ACKNOWLEDGMENTS

I would like to thank the following people for their help: Michael Taylor, for his invaluable editorial contribution and the illustrations; Jack Britton (Principal), for the use of the word processing facilities at the Bristol School of Physiotherapy; Marie-Laurence Viel, for typing the manuscript; Franco Chen, for contributing most of the photographs; Dee Chen for her advice; Sue Paterson, for her helpful comments. And my students and teachers for what they have taught me.

FOREWORD

Despite the rapid increase in popularity and enthusiasm for the art of Aikido in the Western world during the past few decades, there is still too little information available for those who are new to the art.

This is a book written on the subject from two perspectives: one with the eye of wonder of the newcomer, the other from the keen eye of the teacher who guides the newcomer.

The uniqueness of this book may be found in its author who is well-acquainted with Western knowledge in the areas of philosophy, psychology and physiology, and well-integrated with the experience and insight he has gained from the art. This experience, which grows out of his earnest research as a devoted Aikidoist, makes this book much wider and firmer in appeal to the Western mind. In this regard, I recommend highly this book, not only to those who are new to the art, but also to those who teach them.

T.K. Chiba
San Diego, California, USA
January 1991

1
INTRODUCTION

As *ai* (harmony) is common with *ai* (love), I decided to
call my unique *budo* 'Aikido'.

Morihei Ueshiba

MARTIAL ARTS – MYTH AND REALITY

A general survey of definitions of the term martial arts
might reveal a variety of stereotypes. The words themselves imply any skills or techniques employed by the
soldier or warrior with which to fight (Mars being the
Roman god of war). On a more individual heroic level,
cinematic characters of the Bruce Lee ilk are brought to
mind. However, the martial arts hero stereotype is not
restricted to Orientals; the image of James Bond karate-
chopping and kicking his way out of trouble is universally
known. A lesser known and less violent stereotype is of the
bearded sage, who does not seek conflict, but who is able
to defeat an opponent with a deft side-step and a flick of
the wrist. One thing that most, if not all, of the stereotypes
have in common is a personal power of superhuman
proportions, capable of dominating and defeating any
adversary. It is the thought of possessing such a power
that is so alluring to a great number of people, and which
draws so many to a study of the martial arts.

But this great myth, attractive as it may seem, belies a
much greater knowledge; one that is within the grasp of all
who come earnestly to seek it – the knowledge of the self.
At its most profound level, the study and practice of
martial arts may invest in the student not domination over
others, but domination over his own wayward spirit.

Although the term martial arts could literally apply to
all skills designed for fighting or making war, it is generally

1

associated with those arts originating in Eastern Asia. Martial arts is a collective expression for a disparate group of disciplines, which do not really belong in the same category. Furthermore, it is largely a misnomer, coined in the West to apply to an Eastern concept, poorly understood out of that context.

Under the umbrella of martial arts one may include three major general categories:

- Offensive/defensive arts
- Sporting arts
- True *budo*

The distinctions between these three are often blurred, partly as a consequence of their common origin. Actually the second two are progressions from the first. In medieval Japan the manifold fighting arts used offensively and defensively in warfare have given way, in the last two centuries, to the notion of *budo* – a spiritual path of self-realization through conditioning and discipline of the body and mind. *Budo* is a way to end conflict: firstly by defensive techniques designed to disarm and control an opponent; and secondly by creating in the *budoka* (student of *budo*) a peaceful and non-contentious spirit.

The old fighting arts were suffixed by the term -*jutsu*, e.g. *jujutsu*, the supple way (an unarmed fighting style); *kenjutsu*, sword fighting. Where they have evolved to become forms of *budo* they are usually suffixed with the term -*do*. This explanation is somewhat simplistic, for it fails to take into account the corruption of certain *budo* forms to become popular sports (the second item under the general label of martial arts). There had always been a competitive element in the peacetime practice of the old *bujutsu*. Sometimes the outcomes were fatal or resulted in serious injury. To minimize the inherent dangers of these bouts and to modernize them, rules were invented. This also made them viable as spectator sports. The best known of these is judo, which has, for several years, been an Olympic sport.

True *budo* has nothing left in common with these

Morihei Ueshiba, the Founder of Aikido.

Westernized sports, other than a historical tie. This is not to denigrate these other arts, students of which would be the first to admit that what they are practising primarily is a competitive activity. In fact a minority of individuals within these groups prefer to emphasise the *budo* aspects of the art; in so doing, they have retained the traditional elements of etiquette and philosophy, and usually do not participate in competitions.

AIKIDO AS *BUDO*

Aikido is a form of twentieth-century *budo par excellence*. It was the creation of one of the greatest masters of *budo* to have lived – Morihei Ueshiba. Unrivalled in his lifetime in his expertise of martial ways, he was in addition a man of great spiritual and religious yearning. He plumbed the depths of *budo* knowledge, both technical and spiritual; and with an act of genius, single-handedly took the notion of *budo* a quantum leap further up the evolutionary scale. The Founder of Aikido, known as O Sensei (great teacher) to his followers, realized that the essence of *budo* (martial ways) is love: not in some abstract or obscure sense; but loving care for all sentient beings. *Budo* is not a way to make war: on the contrary, it offers a philosophy and a practical means to end strife and resolve conflict. This fundamental notion appears to be misconstrued by many martial artists (students of *budo*), including some students and teachers of Aikido. Some prefer to think of their practice as a way to increase their chances when and if 'push comes to shove'. Some are even prepared to make the initial 'shove' to provoke violence and test their technique. This last, and hopefully small, group is beyond the pale of true *budo*. Even those who strive to increase their own fighting abilities for personal gain, kudos or pride have strayed from 'the Way'.

The Founder's message is crystal clear: we must find a way to end violence and strife, and reconcile ourselves with our enemies. This message, coming from a man who was a giant among martial artists and undefeated in his lifetime, carries even greater weight.

Early in my Aikido career, whilst practising in a *dojo* in San Francisco, I was fortunate to be taught some classes by Terry Dobson, a past student of Ueshiba, in Japan, and now a senior ranking *sensei* of Aikido. He told a now famous story of how once, travelling in the subway in Tokyo, an ugly scene was narrowly averted, although not by his undoubted expertise as an *aikidoka*. A rather drunk and bellicose man boarded the train at one station and immediately began throwing his weight around and abusing passengers. Terry was quite confident of his own ability to subdue the man physically, and was outraged at this anti-social behaviour. He determined to 'put the trouble maker in his place'. Eye contact having been established, a clear message of intent was relayed between them. The man began to approach him, fists clenched, prepared for a fight – a fight that never took place. For suddenly a little old man who had been sitting to one side, reached up and, taking the drunk's arm, gently pulled him down to the seat beside him. In sympathetic tones he asked how he came to be so angry and upset, and gently chided him. The sincerity and obvious concern of the old man's manner soon had the drunk's attention. In a moment he was sobbing out a story of domestic strife, whilst being patted and comforted like a child by the kindly old man. Terry Dobson realized, to his own shame, that he had been prepared to fight this unfortunate person, thereby adding to the conflict. He realized that the old man had demonstrated the true art of *budo*, and that he should look again at his own practice and learn from this experience.

The true student of *budo* practises with all his spirit, mind and body to strengthen them; not to do battle with others, but to do battle with his own ego, to become a mature human being capable of giving love and putting aside self-interest.

MARTIAL ARTS AND THE NEW STUDENT

A senior ranking Aikido master once admitted that many years ago he would rigorously interview all new students, and only those whose motives were of the highest calibre would be accepted to study with him. Since then he had given up setting such severe standards, requiring only that their motives were not of a violent or otherwise criminal nature. He realized that motives are themselves not fixed; they evolve and change with the knowledge and level of development of the student. And this is patently true. There are some who take up a martial art having investigated thoroughly the purpose of *budo* practice. They may have had a background in philosophical or spiritual education. Their approach to practice will initially be quite different from those who started with a desire to keep fit, to learn self-defence or to learn to be assertive; the list is endless. But I would like to suggest that everyone, when considering their motives in retrospect after a few years of practice, would be surprised at the degree to which they have changed, often beyond recognition. Even the philosopher is in for a surprise, for nothing prepares you for *budo* training. The experience is unique, creating as it does an unequalled perspective on life in general and, specifically, on the purpose of training.

I don't wish to discuss here the psychological profile of the typical committed student; what makes him persevere, for example. In fact this may be an interesting area of research for someone, because the drop-out rate for students, especially early on, is remarkably high. Presumably there is a significant disparity between the drop-out's aspirations and expectations and the realities of practice. Unfortunately, unlike James Bond, one does not become a deadly expert after a few weeks of specialist training; no magical powers are acquired overnight, nor even after a lifetime. No doubt there are quite a few students who are disappointed to discover that martial arts training does not fulfil their fantasies, encouraged in part by the media and popular culture. But I am sure that a greater proportion who quit, quite simply find that it was not for them and continue searching for something more suitable.

However, I do strongly suggest to anyone who enters into the *dojo* and on to the mat that they are not hasty. Keep an open mind and do not be put off by the strangeness of the experience. After all, if it were so familiar it would not be so likely to offer you the knowledge and experience you seek.

Given the rather extreme light in which martial arts are often portrayed, it is not surprising that many prospective beginners may doubt their ability to stand up to the rigours of practice. However, accommodation for varying abilities is made in most *dojos*.

When trying to assess your aptitude and capacity for a regular physical regime there are two considerations to be borne in mind: health and fitness. Although inter-related, they should not be confused with each other.

Health

Physical health is primarily concerned with an absence of disease, disability (temporary or permanent) or other sickness. Of course the positive aspect of a sense of well-being is also important.

Ill health is not necessarily a bar to Aikido practice, though it may determine the limit of safe participation. In the first place it is advisable to seek the advice of your doctor if there is any doubt about your ability to practise. But don't forget that although your doctor may be an expert on medical matters, he or she is probably quite ignorant of what is involved in Aikido. In fact, Aikido may be practised very gently, without extremes of aerobic activity or the need to take hard falls. I once practised with a man in his early seventies; an arthritis sufferer. He enjoyed the classes and got a lot from them. Needless to say he practised gently and his fellow students treated him appropriately.

A bit of common sense will decide most cases of doubt. Obviously acute or infectious conditions invariably prohibit practice until they are resolved. However, certain chronic conditions surprisingly may not. The above example of arthritis may be a case in point. Similarly, mild heart conditions, diabetes, epilepsy and many other conditions don't necessarily preclude participation. In all cases, your doctor, *sensei* and fellow students should be informed and if necessary be made aware of how to deal with any acute onset which may occur.

Fitness

Fitness refers to your ability to perform the tasks in question, i.e. it specifically relates to a purpose. Fitness begs the question: fit for what? Poor health, as has been discussed above, may or may not render an individual unfit for a particular training regime. Assuming health is not a problem, you may still be dreadfully unfit, e.g. lacking stamina, strength, suppleness; perhaps also overweight or underweight. These are no reasons to shy away from training. On the contrary, they are often the first reason to get started.

However, it cannot be overstated that you must proceed slowly and gently, building up fitness by gentle increments. Overdoing training in the early stages may not only set you back even further than your starting point, it may deter you for life. 'No gain without pain' is a gross misrepresentation of the truth. Of course you must expect a certain amount of muscle soreness and stiffness, the odd cramp and stitch; but pain is a warning of impending damage, if the damage is not already done.

Learn patience and cultivate respect for your body as you build up your fitness. One day you may be able to tolerate hard training of a kind unthought of today.

If you have any doubts about your suitability for training, seek advice from the *sensei* and your doctor. Then make a decision, being prepared to modify it if necessary. Above all take responsibility for your own body. Injuries and other mishaps are surprisingly rare in Aikido; much less than in competitive sports, contact or otherwise.

Whilst taking the above arguments into consideration,

the obvious positive effects of Aikido training on your health and fitness should not be overlooked. Regular practice can transform your whole being, both physical and mental. Increased suppleness; improved posture, respiration and cardiovascular system; a greater sense of relaxation and well-being are all natural consequences of training. Ill health is much less likely to befall one who is already more resilient and less stressed in this way.

I believe that Aikido is a remedy for the failing spiritual and physical health of people in the modern world; but I will leave the proof of that statement to the reader, should he or she wish to test its veracity through regular Aikido practice.

AIKIDO: THE POTENTIAL

Aikido offers you yourself. This may sound like a *zen koan* or puzzle of great profundity, but it is a simple and straightforward enough statement. The potential is there for you to become a committed *aikidoka*, student and follower of the 'Way' of *aiki*. Do not be put off by the elevated nature of Aikido practice. For you it may be just an opportunity to meet friends and exercise your body in a welcoming atmosphere. Indeed, the Aikido mat is a congenial place. Students practise seriously, but with smiles on their faces and a helping hand for others. You will be made welcome, wherever your motives lie on this spectrum. You will not be judged. But whatever your motives, the practice itself will effect a subtle influence on you and it is impossible to predict where this may lead.

Most *dojos* in Great Britain meet two or three times a week. If your interest and commitment are greater, there is the option of full-time practice. For this it will be necessary to obtain permission to study with a master in one of several locations worldwide. I know of only one full-time *dojo* in Great Britain (part of the British Aikido Federation); apart from this, if you are prepared to visit two or more locations, it is possible to practise daily in some of the larger cities. In most well-established *dojos*, you will find the full range of students, from the casual to the committed. There is no sense of 'one-up-manship' between these extremes. True to the spirit of cooperation inherent in Aikido, students are encouraged to practise and develop at their own pace.

2
HISTORY AND PHILOSOPHY

Aikido cannot be explained with words. One must practise and attain enlightenment of mind and body. Aikido
training is not a sport nor asceticism; it is an act of faith
based on the desire to achieve total awakening. Do not
be in a hurry, for it takes a minimum of ten years to
master the basics and advance to the first rung. Never
think of yourselves as all knowing perfected instructors.
You must continue to train daily with your students
and progress together on the path of *Aiki.*

Morihei Ueshiba

This quote from the Founder is unequivocal. To understand Aikido one must practise it. Words are limited: they
may not be able to explain Aikido, but they can support an
understanding of it. They can also entice the reader to go
on to practise.

The life story of the Founder, and the background
history of Japanese martial arts, can and should be
explained to the new student, as they give valuable
insights into the meaning of Aikido practice today. They
may, hopefully, encourage and instil in the student a
greater sense of courage and stoicism when practice is
hard and morale is low.

Like any great innovator, Morihei Ueshiba was influenced by his predecessors and his peers. He did not
conjure up his unique *budo* from a vacuum. He took knowledge, passed on to him by other masters, who in their turn
were taught by their predecessors; and, not content to rest
with this legacy, he went on to forge a new way to

11

enlighten succeeding generations. His work is part of the flow of history.

The history of Japan is unique and fascinating. Most people have heard of the *samurai* warriors and their almost mythical prowess in battle. But Japan is also known for its profoundly religious culture, so that the term *zen* is at least familiar, even though its meaning is unknown to most people. It was the fusion of these two aspects of Japanese culture that created *budo* or, as we in the West call them, martial arts. If you can grasp to some extent the concept of *budo* you are halfway to a grasp of Aikido, for the latter is a modern form of *budo*, as will be explained later.

But it will also become apparent that Aikido is not a system for fighting, but a Way to self-discovery through physical and martial discipline. For *budo* does not merely describe ways of fighting or defending yourself; underlying the physical practice of techniques is a philosophy relating to life, death and the preservation of peace. To know something of Japanese history will make this more clear. And if an understanding of *budo* helps you to achieve a grasp of Aikido principles, then you may be further helped by an understanding of the Founder of Aikido – his personal history, *budo* training, and philosophy, all of which contributed to his unique and powerful development of *budo*.

As a contemporary *budo* form Aikido owes its existence, in part, to the influence and union of older *budo*, the father of this union being the sword, the mother *jujutsu* (or perhaps *aikijutsu*). Further information on sword arts is given in Chapter 6 on weapons, *aikijutsu* is described in more detail in the history section of this chapter, while for the history and practice of *jujutsu* see page 106.

The word Aikido is in fact composed of three Japanese characters, *ai* meaning harmony, *ki* meaning energy or life force and *do* meaning way or path (with perhaps spiritual connotations). In short, Aikido may be defined as the way of harmony of *ki*. The combined pictograms *ai* and *ki* have a long lineage, dating back to medieval times, but their

合

ai

氣

ki

道

do

contemporary meaning as defined by the Founder of Aikido is radically different to their earlier sense. A brief survey of the history of *budo* will clarify this change from the ancient fighting art of *aikijutsu* to the modern path of enlightenment of Aikido.

THE HISTORY OF *BUDO*

Japanese history is divided into dynasties, each named after emperors or *shoguns*:
- *Nara*   710–94
- *Heian*   794–1185
- *Kamakura*   1185–1336
- *Muromachi*   1336–1573
- *Azuchi-Momoyama*   1573–1603

- *Tokugawa*   1603–1868
- *Meiji*-Restoration   1868–present

Prior to the ninth century AD civil government, and therefore civil servants, held sway over military officials. However, during the Heian period central government became increasingly unable to control certain provincial families, which were becoming more rebellious and warlike as their power grew. To contain these rebellions, other families, notably the Taira and Minamoto, were given control over military matters. These warrior families grew in strength, and, unfortunately for the civilian government, were not content with the authority vested in them; for, having settled the problems in the provinces, they went on to overthrow civilian rule. So began a period of militaristic feudal rule that was to last for centuries.

As power shifted from civilian to military hands so did status. The *bushi*, or warriors, of feudal Japan became a class of men in the ascendant. In these warlike times such personal qualities as loyalty to the family, and skill and bravery in battle, were considered of the greatest value. The seeds were thus sown for the rise of the *samurai* and the principles of *bushido*, meaning literally 'the Way of the warrior'.

Bushido included a code of ethics similar to the notions of honour, bravery and justice of the early English knights. However, unlike the English knights, these ethics were not based on Christian principles, but on a mixture of Shinto, Confucian and Buddhist ideas. Shinto and Confucian notions gave the *bushi* a belief in ancestor respect and filial piety, but it was the incorporation of *zen* Buddhist ideas into their faith that had the greatest impact. With the possibility of death a daily reality, *zen* philosophy offered a point of view creating stoicism and fatalism in the minds of these intrepid warriors.

Consider this quote from the *Primer of Bushido* (credited to Daistoji Yusan):

The idea most vital and essential to the *bushi* is that of death, which he ought to have before his mind day and night ... Consider every day of your life your last and dedicate it to the fulfilment of your duties.

It was *zen*, of which more will be spoken later, that gave the *bushi* a philosophical basis for an indifference to death, a lack of attachment to this material world, and the mind of 'no mind'; all necessary, if one was to face battle and a possible bloody death without flinching.

Besides the prerequisite state of mind, the *bushi* also needed the necessary battle skills to survive in his vocation. *Bushi*, certainly from the Muromachi period, when they were known as *samurai*, were born into the warrior class. Their battle skills were called *bugei*, later known as *bujutsu*, and encompassed a multitude of forms of weapons and empty-handed fighting traditions, some examples including *bo* (a long stave), *so* (spear), *ken* (sword) and *kyu* (bow). Horse-riding skills were known as *bajutsu*, and the empty-handed combat systems of one generic type were known as *jujutsu*.

From the early Heian period to the beginning of the Tokugawa period there were 700 years of feudal warfare that contributed to a growth in the knowledge of the warrior arts, during which time the *bushi* were able to develop their fighting skills. For each weapon or form of *bujutsu*, countless styles or *ryu* (styles or schools) evolved, and these were passed down along 'blood' lines from father to son, through generations. Furthermore, new *ryu* were constantly being created as masters styled their own variations and passed them on to their descendants. It is staggering to consider the countless generations of men living and dying by the sword, the sheer magnitude and intensity of this human creative energy. The development of this body of knowledge known as *bujutsu* is unparalleled in the history of mankind; even the scientific and industrial revolutions, which have changed the face of the earth so radically, are, as yet, relatively short lived by comparison.

Finally, however, the Tokugawa period brought relative stability, after centuries of turmoil. Treaties were made and, as a result, battles were no longer fought; and the *samurai*, the most highly honoured of the non-royal classes, became largely redundant. Their way of life had meant that they were not expected to work in any field save their own profession; and now there was no longer a need for their fighting skills.

Some of them left their patrons, and formed groups of wandering outlaws, known as *ronin*, and engaged in banditry or became mercenaries. However, many began to cultivate the various *bujutsu* as a form of practice. Initially, their intention might have been to maintain their fighting skills through regular non-lethal practice and competition; but the underlying spiritual elements of *bujutsu* that had sustained their forefathers combined with the physical practice to sow the seeds of the transition from *bujutsu* to *budo*. *Bujutsu* had evolved to protect the group cause and, although concerned with methods of fighting, it was, at its highest spiritual level, concerned with stopping warfare, not propagating it. The concern of *budo* was and still is the pursuit of self-perfection, awareness and *satori* (or enlightenment). Although *budo* is mainly a product of the twentieth century, its roots thus lie in the eighteenth-century Tokugawa period, a time of great transition.

But *budo* did not replace *bujutsu*. Even today there are those who still practise more for the sake of perfecting their fighting skills than to polish 'the mirror of their souls'. Obviously the scope for *bujutsu* is severely curtailed in times of peace; but with their greater emphasis on technical and practical efficacy, the *jutsu* forms serve as a kind of genetic pool to maintain the strength of the breed. To clarify this analogy, I suggest that *bujutsu* styles act as a reminder to *budoka* (students of *budo*) not to let their practice degenerate into a kind of superficial mimicry, with no true utility as combat forms.

THE HISTORY OF THE FOUNDER

Morihei Ueshiba, born shortly after the end of the Tokugawa period, came into the world at a most auspicious moment in Japanese history, a period of philosophical reflection following several hundred years of intermittent warfare. As such, it was a perfect time to lay the foundations of a new Way that would contain the essence of the past, yet would show the path clearly forward to the future.

Morihei Ueshiba was born on 14 December 1883 in Tanabe, in the province of Kii. He was the fourth child of five, the only surviving male, and a rather indoor type, inclined towards sickliness. As a youth he was quite bookish and developed an early interest in religious teachings. His father, concerned at his son's poor health and lack of physical hardiness, encouraged him in various physical activities, notably *sumo* wrestling and swimming. Ueshiba's father was quite heavily involved in local politics, and on one occasion some political rivals apprehended his father and attacked him. Ueshiba witnessed the attack and was moved, by a desire to protect his family and himself, to take up the study of *bujutsu.*

At the age of 17 he moved to Tokyo to try his hand at commerce, but after a few months working as a merchant his business failed, and, after contracting beri-beri, he returned home. However, while in Tokyo he used the time well to develop an interest in *jujutsu* (at the Kito *Ryu Dojo*) and *kenjutsu*, i.e. the sword (at the Shinkage *Ryu*). Both of these arts were to have a profound influence on his later work as a creative master of *budo*, i.e. in the creation and formation of Aikido.

A year after moving to Tokyo, he married and shortly thereafter tried to enlist in the army, only to be told he was too short by half an inch. Such was his determination to join, up, though – a desire motivated more by patriotism than a warring nature – that he hung from a tree with weights around his ankles to increase his height. This ploy evidently worked, for he was enlisted the following year and went off to serve in Manchuria in the Russo–Japanese War (1904–1905), excelling in hard training and becoming a master of the bayonet. He was only 5 feet 2 inches in height but he now weighed 180 pounds (in comparison, I am 6 feet tall, fairly sturdily built, and weigh only the same). Myth has it that he was so finely tuned to *ki* energy that he was able to see a shaft of light preceding any bullets that were fired at him, and was in this way able to avoid them and survive.

Three years after signing up he returned home and his father, keen that he should continue his martial arts training, built a *dojo* and enlisted the services of the *jujutsu* master Takaki Kiyoichi to teach his son.

Then in 1912, at the age of 28, he emigrated with 80 other villagers to settle on virgin land being offered by the government on the northern island of Hokkaido. His political influence in the settlement and his physical prowess were by now quite renowned. He was known to accomplish such feats as pulling a horse and a laden cart from a ditch unaided, and single-handedly ripping up and carrying off tree trunks. On one occasion he is known to have seen off three bandits who tried incautiously to assault him.

Three years later he met Sokaku Takeda, grand master of *aikijutsu* (Daito *Ryu*). The origins of his *bujutsu* date back to the twelfth century and to the ancestors of Takeda, but it was Takeda himself who modified and adapted these ancient techniques to form *aikijutsu*. Ueshiba spent one month studying under him, and, as was the tradition at the time, paid individually for each technique that he learned. This, no doubt, proved costly, as he was shown 118 techniques at the time. After that Takeda was invited to teach on several occasions in Ueshiba's *dojo*, and Ueshiba would often accompany him on teaching tours.

Takeda undoubtedly had a profound influence on Ueshiba's early technique and style. Indeed, there are some who say that Aikido is just a modern *do* form of *aikijutsu*. But this is a naïve and simplistic view, for it fails to take into account the technical influence of *kenjutsu* and the very powerful spiritual events that were to take place later on in Ueshiba's life and which were to transform his whole practice.

Ueshiba's father died in 1919, and that same year he left the settlement in Hokkaido for good. Then, in the following year, he met a man who was to help shape his religious and spiritual beliefs in a powerful way. This man, Wanisaburo Deguchi, was a teacher and mystic, and Ueshiba moved to Ayabe to be with him and to study Shintoism and Shamanism. For all its great influence on *budo* in general, *zen* Buddhism was not Ueshiba's chosen religion; he followed Shintoism, which is a religion indigenous to Japan and not imported, as was *zen.*

In 1925, with Wanisaburo and a small group of disciples, he set off for Mongolia in China, to found a new religious sect. The quest was ill fortuned, however, for they were all arrested and sentenced to be executed as spies, and only the swift intervention of the Japanese consul, and perhaps the hand of destiny, saved their lives. So Ueshiba returned to Ayabe, to continue his *budo* teaching.

The year 1925 is perhaps the most auspicious for the birth of Aikido, for it was at this time that Ueshiba experienced a *satori* (or enlightenment) that instilled in him the true purpose of *budo*, which he describes succintly as 'a love to cherish and nurture all beings'. He describes his experience thus:

I set my mind on *budo* when I was about 15 and visited teachers of swordmanship and *jujutsu* in various provinces. I mastered the secrets of the old traditions, each within a few months. But there was no one to instruct me in the essence of *budo*; the only thing that could satisfy my mind. So I knocked on the gates of various religions but I couldn't get any concrete answers.

Then in the spring of 1925, if I remember correctly, when I was taking a walk in the garden by myself, I felt that the universe suddenly quaked, and that a golden spirit sprang up from the ground, veiled my body, and changed my body into a golden one. At the same time my mind became light. I was able to understand the whispering of the birds, and was clearly aware of the mind of God, the Creator of this universe.

At that moment I was enlightened; the source of *budo* is God's love – the spirit of loving protection for all beings. Endless tears of joy streamed down my cheeks.

Since that time I have grown to feel that the whole earth is my house and the sun, the moon and the stars are all my own things. I had become free of all desire, not only for position, fame and property, but also to be strong. I understood, *budo* is not felling the opponent by our force; nor is it a tool to lead the world into destruction with arms. True *budo* is to accept the spirit of the universe, keep the peace of the world, correctly produce, protect and cultivate all beings in Nature. I understood, the training of *budo* is to take God's love, which correctly produces, protects and cultivates all things in Nature, and assimilate and utilize it in our own mind and body.

From this time onwards Morihei Ueshiba's fame began to spread rapidly throughout Japan. In 1927 he moved to Tokyo to open a new *dojo* and many came, wishing to be his students. Famous masters of other *budo* came to visit him, either to witness this new and devastatingly powerful form of *budo* or to train under him. Jigoro Kano, the founder of modern judo, visited him and is believed to have said, 'This is my ideal *budo*, true judo!' Shortly thereafter he sent several of his top judo instructors to learn from him. Some masters even came to challenge him, but he was invincible. Several of the defeated stayed on, to learn from the man who was becoming recognized as the greatest living *budoka*, and perhaps the greatest *budoka* of all time.

The original Hombu *Dojo* was built in 1931. It was nicknamed 'Hell *Dojo*', for at this time Ueshiba was at his most physically powerful, and the training was said to be very 'hard'.

Apart from his own *uchideshi* (live-in students), of which there were 30, and the numerous visiting students, Ueshiba also taught other professions, such as dancers, *sumo* wrestlers and members of the military police. On one occasion 20 of his students, trainees of the Military Academy, tried to get the better of him with a surprise attack as he was leaving after a class. But he is said to have neatly side-stepped their attacks (they were unable even to touch him) and continued on his way home. On another occasion five of the biggest officers tried to restrain him, but he just shrugged them off like flies. He was, to all intents and purposes, beyond the realms of normal human vulnerability. He is once even said to have demonstrated the *ninja* trick of disappearing whilst completely surrounded by a group of students, although it was not a feat he cared to repeat as he said it took five years off his life each time he performed it.

In 1942 he moved to Iwama, where he had a *dojo* and farm, and it was here he set up the Aiki Shrine. Iwama today is still a centre of pilgrimage for visiting *aikidoka* from around the world, for it was here that Morihei Ueshiba fulfilled his dream, combining farming with Aikido teaching and practice, and continuing his religious studies.

The next decade was a very fruitful period, one that saw the consolidation of techniques and philosophy in a form that we now consider to be modern Aikido. The Aikikai was formed in 1945, even though at that time all forms of *budo* were banned as a precautionary measure after the conclusion of the Second World War, this ban being lifted in 1948. Ueshiba's son, Kisshomaru, born in 1921, was now put in charge of the worldwide dissemination of Aikido.

For 20 years or more people had come from all over the world to study under this great master, who even in his 80s was still a marvel to behold. The Hombu *Dojo* was firmly established as the international centre of world Aikido, and O Sensei, now based at Iwama, visited it frequently to teach and guide his followers. Finally, on 26 April 1969, Morihei Ueshiba died of liver cancer, this date now being a day of special practice and remembrance in Aikikai *Dojo*.

Kisshomaru Ueshiba (known as the Doshu) became the

undisputed head of the Aikikai, being the first blood-line descendant of the Founder, and his son, whose title is Waka Sensei, is next in line for this office. Waka Sensei is currently a senior teacher and *shihan* and has visited Great Britain.

PHILOSOPHY OF THE FOUNDER

> Through *budo* I trained my body thoroughly and mastered its ultimate secret; but I also realized an even greater truth ... I saw clearly that human beings must unite mind, body and the *ki* that connects them and then achieve harmony with the activity of all things in the Universe.

Morihei Ueshiba

The traditional religion of Japan is Shintoism and not Buddhism, which was a latter-day importation from China (probably brought there by itinerant monks). Shinto principles are pantheistic, i.e. they are based on the notion of, not one deity, but many, taking the form of *kami* (spirits) inhabiting all things.

Budo, it has been explained, combined concepts of skill and valour in battle with *zen* Buddhist notions relating to life and death. O Sensei was not a Buddhist, but was undoubtedly affected by Buddhist thinking through his martial arts training. However, he did not expect his students to adopt his religious beliefs; Aikido, he stated, was beyond religion. Whatever their beliefs, be they religious or atheistic, he was concerned that his followers understood and adopted the principles of *aiki*. To quote the Founder:

> Aikido is the religion that is not a religion; rather it perfects and completes all religions. From the time that you rise in the morning to the time you retire at night, you must follow the path of *aiki* and pursue the harmonization of the world and its inhabitants.

O Sensei's goal in offering Aikido was far more than just

the passing on of a set of martial arts skills, no matter how revolutionary or effective. He wanted his followers and all humankind to follow the path of *aiki* to discover inner peace and create world peace. But how can the physical practice of any discipline lead to such a spiritual condition of peace and harmony with self and others?

According to the Founder there are three levels of practice to be mastered (which represent the three levels of existence). The first level of mastery is physical. Through repetition of exercises and *kata*, internalization of physical principles is achieved and one develops from novice to skilled artist. The second level of mastery is psychological. It is concerned with developing the will and commitment to continue practice in spite of adversity. It is also concerned with fear and the means to overcome it. The second level builds character. The third level of Aikido is spiritual. It goes beyond technique or even character. It involves the release from form, as the ego-self becomes the egoless self (form, in this context, refers to technique or style). This egoless self has no concern to win or lose. In fact, in the words of O Sensei it is 'invincible, for it contends with nothing'. The three levels of mastery are ultimately achieved by one practice, namely that of Aikido. One is not required to adopt a different practice for each level. One practice suffices; for in fact the three are one.

The three levels of practice correspond to three levels of existence, or worlds. The first world is manifest. It is the world of appearances; the physical, material, technical world. It is the world we all see, with or without training. The second world is hidden. It represents the secret working behind the manifest world. The forces – gravity and *ki* – and the atoms, the constituents of matter, all have their place here. The third world is divine. It is the world of the spirit and of God. But the three worlds are one, in the same way that the three levels of practice are one. And the three worlds are revealed through the path of *aiki*.

Perhaps the potential beginner is daunted by such lofty

ideals, but there is no need to be. You are not expected to swallow wholesale these ideas, nor pledge allegiance to any creed before you are allowed to practise Aikido. The minimum requirement is that you practise with an open mind, a good heart and a respect for the beliefs and ways of others.

Regarding the attitude with which you practise, it should be said that a competitive spirit is detrimental to practice. O Sensei was unequivocal about this:

> From ancient times, *budo* has never been considered a sport. If there are contests we must be ready to kill. Those who seek competition are making a grave mistake. To smash, injure or destroy is the worst sin a human being can commit. The old saying, 'the martial deities never kill', is true. Real *budo* is a path of peace.

The would-be beginner is advised, and may be relieved to discover, that this philosophy is taken to heart by all true *aikidoka*, no matter how committed they are to practice. It creates, on the mat, a wonderful feeling of harmonious cooperation between students.

O Sensei went through many changes as he travelled his own path of *aiki* from birth to death. Even after his *satori* in 1925, when he discovered the 'true purpose of *budo*' as essentially being love in its most cosmic sense, he continued to change and develop. And there is a definite schism between his pre-Second World War and post-war styles. Partly due to his increasing maturity as a man of philosophy, and perhaps due also to a need to conserve energy as his physical strength waned, he moved on from a hard to a soft style. One should not be misled by the terms 'hard' and 'soft'; there was nothing effete or ineffectual about his later Aikido. In many ways it was more powerful, relying less on a finite or physical strength and more on the extension and projection of an infinite source of power – universal *ki*.

What is of interest to note is that the changes that occurred in O Sensei's development are reflected in the different styles of Aikido existing today. Those *shihan* who were mainly influenced by O Sensei's prewar style went on to teach in the same hard fashion; consequently their own students have passed on a similar style. But *shihan* who practised with the Founder after the war, and perhaps till his death, passed on a somewhat different tradition. Students should be aware that there is some contention between these differing approaches, but that it is inconsequential. O Sensei said that form is not the essence of Aikido. Therefore do not be led astray by debates about form. It is important to remain true to the heart of Aikido and to the Founder; to carry on in the Way of *aiki*.

3
THE PRINCIPLES OF AIKIDO

True *budo* is invincible since it contends with nothing.

Morihei Ueshiba

Before embarking on a detailed discussion of Aikido principles I would like to consider the two protagonists in a practice session, because it would be naïve and incorrect to liken them to an attacker and a defender in the generally recognized sense of these words. Neither are they like two competitors in a combative bout or sporting event. Intrinsically linked with their special inter-relationship is the revolutionary contribution that Aikido offers to a strategy for dealing with unprovoked aggression. To illustrate this, two classic responses to an attack are described, and are then compared with a third alternative, the Aikido response.

It should become clear that, to the committed *aikidoka*, the notion of an adversary is inappropriate both in Aikido practice and in daily life. The following quote by the Founder makes this abundantly clear:

There is no enemy ... You are mistaken if you think that *budo* means to have opponents and enemies and to be strong and fell them. There are neither opponents nor enemies for true *budo*. True *budo* is to be one with the universe.

UKE AND NAGE

Aikido is a traditional martial art, the practice of which generally involves two partners, known as *uke* and *nage*, working together. This chapter is about the principles that both *uke* and *nage* must learn and manifest in their practice. Aikido is non-competitive, so at no time are both attacking each other simultaneously. One attacks and is known as *uke*. The other practises the technique and is known as *nage*. Both are practising Aikido. *Uke* does not act as a 'fall guy' for *nage*'s technique. Both are intent on developing their own practice and also that of their partner.

Nage's role
- To resolve the conflict created by the attack in such a way that restores harmony, making full use of the principles of *aiki*. (These principles are described in detail in the latter part of this chapter.)
- To treat *uke* in a non-aggressive and non-competitive way, whilst challenging his practice.

Uke's role
- To attack *nage* sincerely, with a positive intent.

This does not imply aggressiveness or excessive force. On the other hand, *uke*'s attack must be real and not a stage act. The force and speed may be varied to suit *nage*'s level. *Uke* may, however, work at the limit of *nage*'s ability, thereby advancing his practice. Thus if *nage* does not at least avoid the attack, he may receive a blow forceful enough to encourage a greater effort next time. But too fast or forceful an attack may cause *nage* to revert to a more primitive form of response, i.e. one of collapse or resistance.

Ukemi
Ukemi is the practice of receiving *nage*'s technique in a way particular to Aikido. Resistance to a well-executed technique, or collapse on the part of *uke*, may lead to injury. Having given up his balance in the process of the attack, *uke* must endeavour to restore it; at its most basic, this is a simple matter of survival.

Aiki

All of these factors, in essence, boil down to one imperative: to act together to manifest *aiki*, and this will be discussed in more detail later in this chapter.

THREE RESPONSES TO AN ATTACK

Before describing in detail the principles of Aikido, let us consider three archetypal responses to an unprovoked attack. The term 'unprovoked' is used here deliberately, for the true student of Aikido should neither provoke an attack nor, indeed, attack first. In fact the moral high ground adopted by Aikido collapses if the *aikidoka* should once consider inciting violence.

Submission

In this first scenario the one attacked becomes the victim of the attacker. He acts usually from fear, though it might be from a high moral principle, denying the use of violence even for the purpose of self-defence. However, in the more common case of fear the victim will typically freeze, before collapsing under the onslaught of the attack.

Fear and submission come from a sense of powerlessness. The unfortunate result may be to instil in the aggressor a feeling of augmented power. He may then be encouraged to pursue a life of violence, spreading misery and destruction in his path.

Retaliation

Meeting violence with violence may have a limited success, and if the retaliator has a greater power than his attacker he may end the violence in the short term. There are several problems with this response, however, some practical, some moral.

The aggressor may be stronger and be provoked by the retaliation to use even greater force than he initially intended. But even if the retaliation is successful, it may lead to an endless and escalating cycle of revenge. Violence only breeds more violence; it may lead the once peaceful person from a path governed by a sense of justice and fair play to one where the principle of 'might is right' determines behaviour. This is the path of conflict.

The Aikido response

For most people, variations of the first two responses seem to exhaust the possibilities. But the Founder of Aikido realized that true *budo* (martial arts) is not retaliation, but the way to 'stop the spear'. The question is, how can the conflict, created by the unprovoked attack of one person on another, be resolved – restoring balance and harmony, while at the same time avoiding self-destruction or, worse, the escalation of the conflict? The path of *aiki* appears to offer us a solution to the dilemma.

The principles of Aikido, if truly mastered, allow you to avoid self-destruction and to have a choice not to destroy your attacker. Harmony may be restored, and the chain of cause and effect that inevitably leads to further destruction may be broken. The *aikidoka*, if attacked, neither submits nor retaliates. He blends his own *ki* with that of the attacker, literally taking the other's point of view. He becomes one with his aggressor and then imperceptibly guides him away from his path of violence.

MIND–BODY DUALISM

Since the time of the Greeks, Western civilization has evolved the notion of a human being consisting of two essentially different parts: a mind and a body. Descartes, the French philosopher (1596–1650), is most famous for this concept of dualism. Cartesian dualism was, at the time, a brilliant work of logic that has since been questioned by succeeding Western and Eastern philosophies.

Descartes was a devout Christian who attempted, via logic, to prove the existence of the soul and thereby the existence of God. He could not, however, explain how this ethereal immaterial mind could switch the switches and operate the controls of his entirely mechanical body. And yet this notion of ourselves being minds inhabiting bodies is ingrained subconsciously in our language and our culture; so much so that we have entirely independent paradigms – conceptual systems – to describe the world of the body and the world of the mind. For example, the physical principles that govern the workings of all material bodies, including our own – principles such as gravity, mass, centrifugal force – do not apply to our minds, which are without substance.

The dualistic philosophy, unconsciously maintained by our culture, has led to the development of Western science and medicine. We treat our ailing bodies like repairmen fixing a faulty machine, whilst paying lip service to the mind and how it affects and is affected by the body. Thus the so-called psychosomatic (mind–body) illnesses are consigned to the fringe of medicine. To the Westerner it does not inevitably follow that a physical discipline or practice will, *de facto*, develop the mind or spirit. Granted that sporting activities are generally considered to be 'character building'; still, their main function is to promote physical fitness.

In contrast, the dominant Oriental cultures did not follow a comparable path through history. They were not affected by the paradox of dualism, and saw in mankind not two essences, one base and one divine, but one essence that contained, and was contained within, the universe. They see mind and body like heads and tails, inseparable in principle and in practice.

Without this dichotomy between mind and body it is easy to see how such practices as yoga and *budo* were, and are, considered to be means for developing and healing not just the body, not just the mind, but the inseparable mind–body being. Whilst we in the West pray to save our immortal souls and jog to save our sadly mortal bodies, followers of the Way need only follow one path.

Morihei Ueshiba was a profoundly religious man, whose main concern was perfection of the spirit. On this understanding, the practice of Aikido is a means to perfect the spirit through the medium of a physical practice, i.e. the practice of *waza*, techniques or forms. Aikido obeys the laws of the universe, which are fundamentally harmonious, and it is through the practice of Aikido that we come to know those laws, laws that apply equally on the mat and in everyday life.

NAGE: THE PRINCIPLES

Aikido techniques are bound by immutable laws of harmony and non-contention or non-conflict. This places certain constraints on the manner in which *nage* can act in response to an attack from *uke*.

Most of us are familiar with the classic movie scene of the horse-riding cowboy trying to board a fast-moving train. If the train is southbound the rider does not ride north; he rides south, matching his speed to that of the train's. Then he may easily transfer from horse to train. And in doing so he has observed the first two rules of Aikido:

- Get out of the way of the oncoming force.
- Blend yourself with its speed and direction.

Thereafter the analogy breaks down, for once in harmony with *uke*'s attack, *nage* makes use of gyroscopic principles to lead *uke* into a circular or spiral motion, taking him off balance whilst retaining his own balance. *Nage* remains balanced because he substitutes his own centre for the centre of *uke*. *Nage* is like a spinning top, or the calm eye of the tornado, round which *uke* is flung, losing all self-control.

Like the physicist who reduces the universe to matter and force, space and time, in order to study them more easily, let us consider the elements or principles of Aikido as separate entities. They include the following:

- *Hara* (centre) – the 'centre of gravity', from which balance is maintained and the point from which *ki* appears to emanate (see below).
- Development and extension of *ki*. *Ki* is the motive force that enables *nage* to guide *uke* from his intended path on to another, less destructive, one.

- *Tai-sabaki* – the body movements and steps that allow *nage* to adopt correct positioning as the technique unfolds.
- Leading control – skills by which *nage* harnesses *uke*'s movement to his own before finally immobilizing or projecting him with one of the many throws characteristic of Aikido.

Hara

Hara, also known as *tanden* or one-point, corresponds physically to the concept of centre of gravity. Otherwise, though, it is a distinctly Oriental concept.

The centre of gravity of an object is the point about which that object will rotate if spun. It is also the point at which the sum total of the mass of particles making up that object appears to act. In the human body it lies approximately one inch below the navel. However, just as the heart has greater significance for the Westerner than a mere pump supplying blood to the parts of the body, so the *hara* has more than mere physical significance. To the Japanese the *hara* is the source of physical and spiritual balance; it is in fact the seat of the soul or spirit. To develop an awareness and understanding of one's *hara* is, therefore, to develop both physical and spiritual balance.

Most Westerners feel their emotional selves lie within the region of the heart; hence the idea of 'a broken heart' requires no explanation to a member of our culture. Similarly, when pointing to ourselves or each other, we point to this same region of the upper chest. In men especially, we habitually equate a well-developed upper torso, with bulging pectoral, deltoid and bicep muscles, with the peak of human fitness. But this figure of Western physical excellence is top heavy from the Oriental viewpoint; the centre of gravity is too high, due to an overemphasis on upper body bulk. The effect is to make him overall less stable and more easily toppled.

This disparity between the gravity-physical centre and the heart-emotional centre reflects the dualism inherent in Western thought.

Such a dichotomy does not apply with the concept of *hara*. Here, physical and spiritual centre lies at the one point. From this concept it can clearly be seen how a development of the physical centre will simultaneously have consequences for the development or perfection of the spirit; as they are one and the same, cultivating one is tantamount to cultivating both. This notion is exemplified in the practice of *zazen* – zen meditation in which the student focuses on *hara*, breathing from the one point whilst maintaining a perfectly upright and balanced posture.

On the physical plane, the *aikidoka* makes use of *hara* fundamentally for two reasons: to maintain balance; and as a source from which to project *ki*. This corresponds to the physical concepts of centre of rotation and centre of mass. The earlier description of *nage* avoiding *uke*'s attack, blending with *uke*, then leading him in a circle or spiral, only functions if the centre of mass of the pair, as they revolve, is the centre of *nage*, i.e. *nage*'s *hara*. And this is necessary to fulfil the two conditions, that *uke*'s balance is lost whilst *nage*'s is maintained.

The power that *nage* makes use of in an Aikido technique does not, strictly speaking, emanate from muscle power. In action, a strong upper body musculature is slow and tends to lack both coordination and sensitivity. Furthermore, as it stems from a point above the *hara*, it applies a turning force, tending to topple *nage* over. In Aikido the upper body is relaxed, yet alive; it acts more like a conduit for the flow of *ki* that surges from the *hara*. *Nage*'s mass, acting from his centre, is the motive force driving the technique. *Nage* thus moves from his *hara*, extends *ki* from his *hara*, and spins *uke* around his *hara*. Finally, he always returns to his *hara*, the source of personal *ki*, balance and harmony.

It cannot be over-emphasised that, without a well-developed awareness of *hara*, Aikido cannot be practised correctly or effectively.

Ki (kokyu)

According to the Founder, *ki* is 'the subtle energy which propels the universe'. Practice of Aikido, on the mat, is concerned with the understanding and development of *ki*.

Some schools of Aikido make it their explicit intention to develop *ki*, almost for its own sake, and a large portion of each class is taken up with *ki* exercises; one student tries to unbalance, or tip, his partner, whilst the other concentrates on his *hara*, extending *ki* through his lower limbs to earth and through his fingertips to infinity. There are recorded examples, including on film, of the Founder's students testing their master in this way, without the least success; he was, to all intents and purposes, as solid and immovable as a mountain when he chose to be. However, followers of Ueshiba's Aikido only rarely practise in this way; it is generally accepted that knowledge of *ki* evolves naturally, and is implicit in the practice of Aikido, without excessive attention to tests of *ki*.

Acceptance of the concept of *ki* does not require any commitment to a belief in mystical forces that appear to defy common sense or natural laws. It does require open-minded acceptance of a different, and at first strange, way of using the body. Physically strong individuals often have trouble in Aikido practice; they often attempt, from long-established habit, to substitute the force of their own muscles for the subtle energy that propels the universe. If they would but let go of their desire for control and allow *ki* to flow through them, they might discover that *ki* could also propel their own techniques with far greater effectiveness.

In Aikido, *ki* is expressed as *kokyu* or breath power. The concept of life is almost synonymous with that of breath. So it is small wonder that *ki* energy, which gives life to the universe and man, is equated with *kokyu*. Respiration, in biological terms, refers to both the act of inhalation and exhalation (external respiration) and the oxidation of carbohydrates to release energy to drive the biochemical and biomechanical machine (internal respiration). The vital signs of life, as any medical student will tell you, are pulse and breath.

Kokyu-ho is the act of breathing in time with the universe. As *ki* flows through the universe in a pulsing wave of expansion and contraction, so we inhale and exhale. When practising Aikido, a class often begins with gentle deep breathing exercises coordinated with arm movements, which stimulate the flow of *kokyu* through the body. Then at all times, sitting, standing, throwing or being thrown, *kokyu* should be flowing through the body. It is *kokyu* that gives power to the throw and not the force of contracting muscles.

The feeling of *kokyu* is one of a heavy momentum (a compound of mass and velocity) imparting an impulse of energy from *nage* to *uke*. Muscle power serves only to stifle this flow, as it physically restricts a free-flowing movement. Partners must be free of all upper-body physical (muscular) and mental tension when practising. It is impossible to describe adequately the feeling of *kokyu* flowing through the body to another. It must be felt and experienced and developed through long hard practice. But I can attest to its existence. However, it was several years before I was aware of its fleeting presence in my practice.

In fact all of us have experienced *kokyu* as babies. All babies, being in their natural state, manifest *kokyu*. The grip of a newborn baby is strong enough to support its own weight. Its limbs, when extended, are almost impossible to bend, without injury. When a young child crawls over your back, sits in your lap, or pushes against you, the feeling has a unique quality. One is aware of a non-intrusive energy, compelling but without conflict.

This ability to influence another's behaviour through a subtle application of *kokyu* is a key to good practice. Receiving the technique, one feels an accord, a willingness to comply, or go along with the technique. Applied with force, the same movement may arouse discord, aggression and an instinctive desire to resist the movement.

Good Aikido appears effortless. One who practises using *kokyu* preserves his energy, preferring to channel *ki* through his body. One who uses strength limits his ability and ends up exhausted and spent. The lesson is a simple one, but hard to learn.

Tai-sabaki

Every martial art has its own unique forms of posture and movement, and Aikido is no exception, the art of body movement being called *tai-sabaki*. However, both the posture and movements of Aikido, whilst unique in their developed forms did, in fact, evolve from other *budo* studied by the Founder (namely *kenjutsu, aikijutsu*).

At its highest level, the level of *takemusu* (literally, martial creative) Aikido is formless. *Takemusu* must be our ultimate goal; but it stands forever on the horizon. The further we advance, the further it recedes. Our daily practice, which consists of the repetition of basic forms, may be likened to the *zen* student who tries to achieve *satori* (enlightenment) by solving a *koan* (riddle). Although *koans*, by their nature, have no logical solution, all the avenues of logic must be pursued and exhausted before enlightenment is finally achieved through a direct and intuitive insight. But there are no shortcuts to this realization.

Consider, first, the posture or stance adopted in Aikido. This posture is based on a sword stance, and the Japanese word for this is *hanmi*. The *aikidoka* may stand in either left *hanmi* or right *hanmi*. In right *hanmi* the right foot is forward and turned slightly out from the forward line of attack, the right knee is bent, the left foot is behind the right foot pointing at an angle of about 60 degrees to the line of attack. The left knee is straight, the hands lie in the centre line, fingers extended at and above the level of the *hara*. The back is straight, shoulders relaxed, with 60 per cent of the body weight on the leading foot.

This is a stable posture, on a triangular base, but one from which rapid forward, backward and turning movements can be made. However, whatever movements may intervene, the *aikidoka* always returns to this basic posture. Apart from its inherent stability and natural advantages for rapid movements, it is also a defensive posture, in that the groin is protected by the oblique angle of the stance. This oblique angle also makes the *aikidoka* a narrow target, with the chest and abdomen protected by the leading shoulder, arm and side of the body. *Hanmi* is the point of departure from which the technique begins in basic practice. In more advanced practice stasis is rare, but if you were to 'freeze frame' a film of Aikido in motion you might observe that the basic posture of *hanmi* is still adhered to.

There are two fundamental steps in Aikido that form the basis of all movements: *irimi*, an entering step; and *tenkan*, a turning step. Simple as these two steps may appear, they interact in various combinations to form a complex and sophisticated pattern of movements that tends to baffle most beginners in their first few months of practice.

Irimi evolved from Ueshiba's expertise with the bayonet and later with the *jo*, and formed the basis of his early practice of Aikido. A decisive and forceful entering step, *irimi*, preempted any notion of attack by *uke*, returning his force back on himself with a swift blow (*atemi*) or throw. *Tenkan* evolved later. A simple *tenkan* movement is similar to the matador's pirouette as the bull charges through. In this way a forceful strong attack by *uke* is avoided initially, then led in a circle or spiral about *nage*'s centre as *nage* completes the *tenkan* movement.

Both these movements are similar in principle to those employed in the art of *jujutsu*, thus highlighting the common origins of these two arts. In *jujutsu* one learns to push when pulled and pull when pushed; in Aikido one enters when pulled and turns when pushed.

Irimi, if practised correctly, is a devastatingly conclusive movement when coupled with *atemi* or a throw. The movement requires accurate timing and a sixth sense to preempt an impending attack. Even so, one does not enter directly but moves slightly off the line of *uke*'s projected attack. The attack is thereby avoided, whilst at the same time *nage* is in an ideal position to take advantage of the opening created in *uke*'s defence. From this position of obliquity, be it in front or behind *uke*, a blow or throw is far more likely to unbalance *uke* than one carried out from a point directly in front. The principle of *irimi*, fundamental to Aikido, dispels any false notion that Aikido is purely a reflexive art requiring *uke* to initiate the attack. Using the principle of *irimi*, an impending attack may be dealt with decisively before it is launched.

Tenkan, used alone, is a reflexive movement and may be an appropriate response to a strong unanticipated attack. *Tenkan*'s circular movement allows *nage* to avoid, then absorb, *uke*'s attack; it also allows *nage* to deal with an extremely strong attack. The linear energy from the attack is transformed into circular momentum, *nage* being positioned at the centre of this circle. *Nage* extends *ki* from a well-balanced *hara* and, making use of leading control (to be discussed in the next section), is able to control *uke*'s movement. *Nage* may then determine the outcome of the encounter, without the need to suffer or inflict injury.

Combining the movements of *irimi* and *tenkan* was an act of genius by the Founder of Aikido, as it added a completely new dimension to the practice. *Irimi-tenkan* allows *nage* to enter decisively, taking *uke*'s balance; then, turning rapidly, *nage* can absorb the force of *uke*'s attack. This simple, yet revolutionary, combined movement opens the door to a variety of options and outcomes. It not only allows *nage* the possibility of increasing his own chances of survival, but allows for an increase in those of *uke* also.

Irimi-tenkan, in fact, is unique to Aikido, and played a key role in the evolution of the art from its predecessors such as *jujutsu*.

Aikido, it has been said, is an ideal defence against a multiple attack. This ability to deal with more than one assailant came about as a direct result of the evolution of *tai-sabaki* from *irimi* and *tenkan*, to *irimi-tenkan*.

Irimi may be used against a single attacker. A swift entry with a strong technique and the outcome is decisive. However, if there are two attackers, *nage*'s back is left unprotected with a single *irimi* movement. *Tenkan* overcomes this difficulty. It allows *nage* to deal with the first *uke*, and at the same time to turn and face the second. *Nage* may even use the body of the first *uke* as a shield or projectile against the second.

Combining *irimi* and *tenkan* allows *nage* to move and to turn in any direction, unpredictably and at speed. With this ability, *nage* can theoretically defend himself against a multiple attack. Like a whirlwind in a cornfield, the *aikidoka* has the capacity to move here and there, drawing the attackers into a spinning vortex, then flinging them out. The attackers will probably collide with each other in their attempts to pin down or strike *nage*; but the latter is never static, always elusive. To use yet another metaphor, *nage* is the conductor of the orchestra of which the attackers are the musicians. The conductor leads and controls the group with the baton; he literally calls the tune and determines the final cadence.

Having absorbed basic *tai-sabaki* principles, the *aikidoka* goes on to incorporate these movements into sometimes elaborate choreographies of circular and spherical motion.

Leading control

Having achieved a state of *aiki* with *uke*, *nage* must then lead him to completion of the technique, completion in this case referring to either an immobilization (pin) or a projection (throw). Leading control refers to the way in which *uke* is drawn from his intended path on to one determined by *nage*. In accordance with *aiki* principles, the lead must be without a sudden clash or conflict. *Uke* is hardly aware that a change has taken place; it is something like a train switching tracks. Leading control makes use of physical and psychological principles, the latter being the basis of the 'touchless' throw, a seemingly impossible feat of which Ueshiba was a master. But there is no magic to this, for one may lead the body or the mind or both. If I held out a £5 note for you to take, and then snatched it away before you were able to grasp it, you might stumble, but you would probably draw back at the last moment. If, however, with perfect timing, I drew my hand away like the matador's cape, just ahead of your reaching hand, you would overreach yourself, barely aware of what was happening; subconsciously your mind would be led by mine as it continued to believe the note was almost within its grasp. The reflex to withdraw would not be initiated until perhaps too late, and you could find yourself toppling to the ground, unbalanced by your own intention and the leading control exerted, not on your body, but on your mind.

Leading control by physical means requires a minimum of force. In Aikido, *uke*'s movement in a straight line is diverted by *nage* into a circular or spiral movement. As already described, *nage*'s *hara* is the centre of that circle. Applying *ki* energy obliquely to *uke*'s body, he will be drawn into a circular path around *nage*. His awareness of the change will be minimal, and probably too late, because of the subtle and non-intrusive manner in which it has been carried out.

Nage thus learns simultaneously to lead both the mind and body of *uke*. Like learning to ride a horse, the skills required take time to learn, but there is no limit to the degree of mastery you can achieve if determined to practise regularly and diligently. *Uke* is not just a body moving under physical laws; he also has a mind, which may change at the slightest whim. The good *aikidoka* effectively uses the principles of both physics and psychology.

Through a sound understanding of leading control, *nage* controls *uke*'s attack, the technique being concluded by *uke* either being immobilized with a pinning technique or being thrown. The immobilizations and projections which constitute the basis of Aikido *waza* (techniques) are outlined in Chapter 4.

UKE: THE PRINCIPLES

So far we have discussed *nage*'s role in Aikido practice. *Uke*'s role is twofold: to attack *nage*; and to survive, uninjured, the inevitable response to that attack.

The attack

Since Aikido is non-competitive, *uke* and *nage* must therefore alternate roles. *Uke* normally makes one attack that must be dealt with by *nage*. Occasionally practice involves *uke* countering *nage*'s technique; but this form of practice is rare, for it should be borne in mind that a well-executed technique should not leave any opening that might be countered. *Uke* learns to attack using *hara* and *kokyu*; he does not attack in an uncontrolled aggressive manner. However, the attack must be sincere and carried out with real intent. Without bearing any ill-will towards his partner, nor desire to better him, *uke* gives *nage* an opportunity to develop his practice and test his skills. The attack may be slow at first, or when working with beginners; but even so it should carry the full weight of *uke*'s intent.

This manner and philosophy of attack are common to most *budo*. Generally, students of *budo* are taught devastatingly efficient and sometimes lethal blows that are executed in a manner of concentrated meditation. Blows are not struck in anger or for personal gain; they are, at the least, a last resort in self-defence and, at most, a method to develop one's spirit and to assist one's partner in the pursuit of the same.

Ukemi

Ukemi is the art of restoring balance and thereby surviving *nage*'s response to an attack. For example, in the case of a throw, *uke*'s balance is first taken, and he is then led in a circular or spiral direction and projected across or down on to the mat. *Uke* must not only escape injury but also return quickly to a state of balance and readiness in preparation for further encounters.

When we fall or are thrown on to the ground, several possible outcomes exist. If we stay relaxed and fall without twisting or trapping a limb, we may escape with a few bruises; like the Saturday-night drunk who, falling like a sack of potatoes, escapes serious injury. Still, this is a form of collapse that leaves us vulnerable to further attack;

although we may have survived the throw, we have not restored our own balance and are unable to continue in our role as *uke*. Alternatively we may tense up from apprehension or fear. Although it appears instinctive to do this, such a response is very dangerous, and the likelihood of injury greatly increased. A tense body cannot absorb an impact safely and the energy imparted to a stiff body is likely to cause damage to joints or possible bone fractures.

The *aikidoka* learns, on falling, neither to collapse nor to become stiff. He maintains normal muscle tone, extending *ki* through the fingertips. He allows his body to move in a circle about his *hara*; this is the direct analogue of *nage*'s role. The linear force of the throw is converted into circular energy. In this way *uke* uses *nage*'s force to restore his balance by the simple expedient of rolling forwards or backwards until once more on his feet (see photograph on page 55).

My own *sensei* considers *ukemi* to be of paramount importance, perhaps because it requires the most courage to perform well and therefore strengthens and develops the spirit. Perhaps also because *ukemi* is analogous to life's trials. How should we deal with adversity? By collapsing in a heap, unable to go on, or tensing with fear, only to break when struck? Perhaps we can learn to blend with adversity and restore our balance, making use of the very forces that knock us down.

SEIZA

The seated position of *seiza* embodies, in static form, the principles that have been described thus far. *Seiza* is the traditional way of sitting in Japanese society (see group photograph on page 46). It is also a position of meditation. It is a position of balance and stability. The base is a solid triangle, with the two knees as two corners and the feet, heels together, as the third. The body in this position forms a pyramid, with the crown of the head as the apex; and, as the ancient Egyptians were patently aware, the pyramid is probably the most stable and solid structure that can be devised. Combining the physical properties of the *seiza* position with a well-grounded centre creates in the individual a real sense of almost indestructible equilibrium. I have seen a film of the Founder in which several of his students tried to tip him over whilst he sat in *seiza*. Though quite advanced in years at the time, a group of strapping young *aikidoka* were unable to budge him one inch. So united was his *ki* with that of the universe, it must have been like trying to move a mountain.

To adopt the *seiza* position correctly, building on the triangular base, you sit back on your heels. The spine extends vertically, stretching up toward the sky. The crown of the head pushes upwards with the chin retracted, the shoulders and arms relaxed, with the hands resting on the thighs. Breathing gently through the nose, the eyelids are narrowed and awareness is focused on the *hara* and, from this point outwards, encompasses the immediate surroundings. Personal *ki* energy is connected, via the earth, with universal *ki*. *Ki* also extends from the *hara* and up through the spine and out of the crown of the head, down through the arms and out of the extended fingertips. Maintaining this position, the breathing should be regular and gentle, and the posture perfectly vertical.

Seiza practised in this way is synonymous with *zazen* (*zen* meditation, or literally 'sitting-*zen*'). Through the practice of *zazen*, enlightenment is realized through posture and breathing, the basis of this philosophy being that human beings do not have to seek enlightenment as they are already enlightened. According to *zen* philosophy, enlightenment is a result, not of action or achievement, but of allowing your mind to blend with the universal mind. By adopting *seiza* posture, you are simply in a state of timeless being or oneness with universal *ki*.

Seiza is the position adopted by *aikidoka* on the mat at all times when they are not engaged in dynamic practice. Whilst sitting in *seiza*, however, you still continue to practise Aikido. At all times, whether moving or still, the *aikidoka* demonstrates harmonization of personal and universal *ki*. When the mind is open to this realization it becomes clear that Aikido is the practice of moving *zen*, whilst *seiza* is that of sitting *zen*.

4
PRACTICE

Words and letters can never adequately describe
Aikido. Its meaning is revealed only to those who are
enlightened by hard training.

Morihei Ueshiba

Aikido is practised in a hall known as a *dojo*. The class is
led by the *sensei* (literally, one born before). The manner
of practice may seem strange at first to the newcomer; a
certain formality appears to underlie all activities within
the *dojo*. So some explanation of why and how these activities are conducted may help to allay the apprehensions
of the beginner.

First, it should be realized that the word 'practice' has a
quite distinct meaning when applied to Aikido. This
meaning derives from *zen* philosophy and is used in much
the same way in most *budo*.

We in the West tend to think of practice as a means to
an end. Practice, it is said, makes perfect. In this sense
practice merely serves as a vehicle to improve our technique. Perfection or, at least superiority, is our goal. In
most fields of activity this superiority is rewarded,
perhaps with trophies, financial gain, or at least popular
acclaim.

In *zen*, however, it would be more accurate to say that
practice is perfect. All activities have inherent value: no
extrinsic purpose is sought. It is important to practise,
concentrating on the now, to realize the self fully.
Emphasis is placed on right attitude when practising.
Without thought or gain, we focus on each activity as it
occurs, giving all our attention and spirit to this one act.
Those wishing a deeper understanding of this concept of
practice should consult the many good texts which exist on
zen and *budo* philosophy.

Group photograph of teacher and students at Chiba Sensei's *dojo*. The author is standing directly behind Chiba Sensei in the centre of the picture.

The following descriptions inevitably make more sense when viewed from this perspective. The formality is not mere form; it is not designed to constrain the individual but, on the contrary, to liberate him or her.

THE *DOJO*

The *dojo* is the place of practice for martial arts or *budo*. Its literal meaning is the place where one studies and practises the Way. The same word is also generally applied to the place of *zen* meditation; though in the latter case the word *zendo* may equally be applied. In this country the actual location of the *dojo* may be a hall of any kind (sports, church, community, etc.), where the mats will probably be laid out before each class and put away between classes. In rare cases there may be a permanent *dojo*, with fixed mats. The advantages of the latter are many; but in any case, whether the *dojo* is permanent or temporary, a respectful attitude is expected.

Aikido, unlike some *budo*, involves throws and falls. Therefore, to ensure the safe practice of *ukemi*, it is practised on a mat and not on the bare floor. The type of mat varies, but is usually an area consisting of individual 6 × 3-foot segments, thick enough and dense enough to absorb the impact of a body falling at speed. Sometimes a canvas is stretched over the mat, giving a smoother more even surface on which to practise. In the middle of one edge of the mat there is often a small table, on which a photo of the Founder is placed, and perhaps a small vase of flowers or incense. This is known as the *kamiza*, and is a point of orientation for practice. Usually the edge opposite the *kamiza* is where students enter or depart from the mat, leaving their sandals on the way. The *sensei* enters or leaves from one of the side edges.

Care of the *dojo* is an important part of Aikido practice. It may involve daily sweeping of the mat, dusting the *kamiza*, replacing flowers, etc. Care of the *dojo* is necessary not only for hygienic reasons; it is also a measure of respect and helps develop a right sense of 'place'.

The *dojo* is more than just a training hall for development of bodily arts. To quote Shihan T.K. Chiba, 'It is a place where severe and intense destruction of the ego takes place.' Though one hesitates to call it a place of worship, still it is a place of spirit.

SENSEI

The *sensei* is the teacher of the *dojo*. O Sensei (literally Great Teacher) is the name given solely to Morihei Ueshiba, the Founder. Aikido is the practice of the Way of *aiki*. By the same token, the *sensei* is one who is further along this Way than his students. His role is to enable them to find their Way, by guiding their practice.

But it must be remembered that all *aikidoka*, *sensei* and students alike, are followers of the Way. Each has his or her own path to follow, which is sacred. The *sensei* is also a student, as practice is lifelong. Even so, the relationship between *sensei* and students is governed by traditional

47

etiquette, being based on mutual respect; on the mat, the *sensei*'s word is final and no debate should arise between students, and certainly not between student and *sensei*.

Furthermore, the *sensei* will invariably be a student of one who is of higher rank. The latter may possibly be a *shihan*, a term reserved for high-ranking masters, who in many cases were students of O Sensei. Ideally, an unbroken line of ascendancy connects the first-time beginner with the Founder of Aikido.

DRESS AND APPEARANCE

The traditional dress for practice is a judo *gi* (or suit), with an *obi* (belt) denoting rank. A white *obi* denotes all grades below *dan* grade; a black *obi* denotes all grades from *shodan* (first *dan*) upwards. In some schools coloured belts are worn to denote rank, from beginner to *dan* grade, but in the main only white or black belts are worn.

The *gi* consists of white baggy cotton trousers, usually strengthened at the knees, and a strong loose white cotton jacket that will not tear when gripped or pulled repeatedly. When buying a *gi* it should be remembered that the material will shrink, usually about 2 inches in the sleeve and leg. Ideally, the wrists should be exposed for gripping attacks and the trousers should end above the ankles, to avoid the toes getting caught. Make sure you buy a good quality judo *gi* and not a lighter-weight *gi* as used in some other *budo*, as these may quickly become worn out or torn. A *gi* can be bought in many of the better stocked sports shops, martial arts shops, or often through the *dojo*. This last source is often the cheapest option. An average price for a *gi* is £30 (1991 prices). You might need two if you practise frequently; but they should last at least two years. If you are prepared to patch the knees on the trousers, they will last a lot longer.

Dan-grade students wear a dark blue or black *hakama* over their white trousers. This form of dress was the traditional wear of the *samurai*, and consists of a divided and pleated skirt-like apparel, with long belts which wind round the waist. The movement and feel of the *hakama* adds grace and, some may say, beauty to the flowing spiral-like movements of Aikido.

The *hakama* and the *obi* are tied at the level of the *hara*, i.e. just below the navel, as this gives the *aikidoka* a strong awareness of his centre. For women students, however, this is not possible, as their wider hips and narrower waists make it necessary to tie their belts at the level of the waist.

Sandals are worn to the mat, but practice on the mat is barefoot. Headbands, bright flashy decals and other such items that draw attention to the self are avoided; rings and other jewellery are removed for similar reasons and for safety's sake. The overall appearance is one of modesty, with a minimum of personal style. Fingernails and toenails should be kept short to avoid injury, the hair should be tied back if long, and the body and clothing should be clean. Expanses of hairy chest are considered unseemly. Of course dress may become disarranged during practice but it should be adjusted frequently. Women will need to wear a tee-shirt under the jacket of their *gi*.

ETIQUETTE

Etiquette describes the rules of acceptable behaviour in the *dojo*. Some people may feel that the observance of a set of formal rules is somehow demeaning. To allay their apprehensions, an explanation of the nature and reason for traditional etiquette may be helpful.

Firstly, *budo* etiquette is not mindless. In fact the reverse is true. It is a functional part of practice, and as such it is carried out mindfully with full awareness and concentration.

Secondly, etiquette serves to lift you out of your everyday mind, full of mundane cares and concerns, to a level, where, for the period of the class, your one concern is 'right practice'.

Thirdly, etiquette allows a formal recognition of respect for, and gratitude to, your partner and *sensei*, for making the practice possible. Respect and gratitude are of course mutual, and the *sensei*, whatever his status or rank, is bound by the same rules of etiquette as the complete novice.

By adhering to formal rules of etiquette you will be constantly reminded that you are practising a martial art and that personal feelings must be kept under control. Were this not the case, you may forget that your partner offers his body willingly and freely to assist you, and that anger or desire to dominate the other should never be a factor in your practice.

As with all etiquette, some variation may exist between *dojos* and usually depends on the *sensei*'s previous experience. Form is not rigid, and neither is there necessarily strict conformity with tradition.

Rei

The single most repeated act of etiquette in Aikido is the *rei* or bow. A standing *rei* is a bow performed from the waist, with the back straight and the palms of the hands resting on the front of the thighs. Eye contact is maintained with your partner and you avoid exposing the back of the head and neck, as these are vulnerable areas to a possible attack. This tradition dates back to a time when offering the back of the neck, even in a formal situation, was a potentially suicidal error of judgment.

The *rei* may also be performed from a kneeling position (*seiza*). Bowing forward from the waist, the left hand is placed on the mat palm down. The right hand is placed next to it with the tips of the thumbs and index fingers touching. This forms an inverted spade shape in the space bound by index finger and thumbs. Again eye contact is maintained whilst the *rei* is performed. Returning to an upright posture the hands are removed in reverse order (right first) and placed on the thighs.

New students often ask what is the purpose of the *rei*. Perhaps in their minds there lies a doubt and reluctance to bow to another person, since in the West this implies a form of subservience, a throwback to our feudal past. However, the tradition arises from Japanese culture, where the *rei* is used as a form of greeting, farewell, thanksgiving, and a sign of mutual respect. In Japan the boss bows to the employee on the shop-floor, and vice versa. No implication of superiority is intended. If O Sensei were here today he would bow to a beginner, since he himself would be equally bound by the rules of good manners.

Bowing on entering and leaving the mat, you are signalling your respect and reverence of the *dojo* in which you practise. Bowing to a fellow student, you are asking that he will practise with you and you are signalling that you will take care of his person throughout the interchange. The *sensei* bows to a student when he greets him or requires him to assist in a demonstration of a technique.

The action of *rei* is thus a constant reminder to make and keep you forever mindful in your thoughts and actions. It assists you, so that you do not fall into sloppy practice. This way you will stay centred and sharp, like the blade of a *samurai* sword. One day your life or another's may depend on this. In the meantime, sloppy practice means you have slipped from the Way.

Entering and leaving the *dojo* and the mat

Practice begins at the point of entry to the *dojo* and continues until the *dojo* is vacated.

On entering the *dojo* the *aikidoka* makes a standing *rei* in the direction of the *kamiza*. This action signals the beginning of practice. The correct form for this is zarei. It effectively states that you are aware of the place in which you stand and that you are prepared to begin practice. Leaving the *dojo* the *rei* is also performed, for similar and complementary reasons.

Usually there is an area of floor adjacent to the mat where personal belongings may be left. The *aikidoka* then approaches the edge of the mat. If the class has already begun, you should await a signal from the *sensei* before stepping on to the mat. Otherwise, you make another standing *rei* to the *kamiza* before removing your sandals and stepping on to the mat. This last action is best performed by turning your back to the mat and slipping the sandals off so they are neatly placed together and ready to be put on when leaving. Turning to face the *kamiza*, the *aikidoka* adopts the position of *seiza* by bending first the left knee then lowering the body with back straight and vertical until the left knee is on the mat. Then the right knee joins the left. A kneeling *rei* is then performed to the *kamiza*. The reverse sequence of events occurs as the *aikidoka* leaves first the mat and finally the *dojo*.

ON THE MAT

Though variation inevitably does occur between *senseis* and from one class to the next, a common pattern or structure is usually adhered to.

The beginning

If a class is about to begin, students line up in *seiza* opposite the *kamiza*, with senior students at the right (facing the *kamiza*). Prior to this time students may perform their own warm-up exercises, or practise whatever they choose alone or with a partner. Classes usually start punctually and students should be prepared for this moment, i.e. lined up quietly in *seiza*.

The *sensei* will then enter the mat, following the same etiquette as the students, though usually from a different side of the mat. He walks quickly to a point in front of the *kamiza* and sits in *seiza*. He may sit facing the students. This may be followed by a minute or two of meditative silence. He will then turn to face the *kamiza* and, in synchrony, everyone performs a *rei* to the *kamiza*. This formally begins the class, and acts as a mark of respect and gratitude to the Founder for the gift of knowledge; it is not a form of religious subservience to a graven image, but a form of remembrance. The *sensei* then turns, and a simultaneous *rei* is performed between *sensei* and students. The words 'Onegaishimas' is said at the same time; roughly translated, it means 'please practise with me'.

The warm up

After 'bowing in', there follows a period of warm-up exercises in which students copy the *sensei*'s movements. The exercises prepare the students physically and mentally for the paired practice, and help to remove tension from stiff muscles. Many of the exercises are common to other martial arts, and fall into the following categories:

* Breathing exercises
* Moving exercises
* Stretching

Students learn a series of breathing exercises, usually coordinated with arm movements. The principles of breathing have been known for thousands of years by the ancient *yogis* of India, who understood that they were fundamental to a healthy existence. This knowledge has filtered down into martial arts practice.

Breathing slowly and deeply through the nose, into the *hara*, the arms are raised slowly. At the peak position of the arms the in breath is maximal. The arm-raising serves to mobilize the ribcage and assist greater lung expansion. Pushing gently down into the *hara* with the diaphragm, the breath is held for about two seconds. Then, slowly, the arms are lowered as the air is gently expelled to a maximum out breath. This sequence may be repeated for about two minutes.

The effects of deep controlled breathing are very beneficial to the mind and the body. Calm concentration is instilled in the mind, while the body musculature relaxes. Increased oxygenation of the blood and increased blood flow stimulate the tissues to great vigour. Toxins are removed more quickly by the blood, and the whole body is put in a state of relaxed readiness for action.

Breathing exercises, in fact, are used to great effect in Aikido to promote the flow of *kokyu* through your system, by breathing life from the core of the *hara* to the tips of the fingers and toes and beyond.

In the moving exercises the arms are rotated windmill fashion, the spine is rotated gently and the torso bends forwards, then backwards, then from side to side. All parts of the body are thus involved, gently mobilising the joints, increasing flexibility and promoting good blood flow to the soft tissues surrounding the joints and to the muscles. These exercises generate heat and so the body literally warms up throughout this process.

Stretching exercises are done preferably when the body is already warmed up; stretching cold muscles may be damaging as they are less pliable in this state. Stretching should always be done gently and without force; and so-called 'ballistic' stretching, i.e. bouncing on the stretched muscles, is to be avoided at all costs. This is, firstly, because it only stimulates a reflex in which the muscle contracts, thereby defeating the purpose of the stretch; and, secondly, because bouncing on a fully stretched muscle is likely to tear it, especially if it is cold. These tears may only be tiny micro-tears, but, even so, may lead to adhesions (small scars), which tether the muscle and reduce its ability to stretch.

The correct method of stretching is slowly and gently to take the muscle to a point where it begins to feel tight, then to hold the position whilst gently breathing and concentrating on letting go of tension. After about 10 seconds the muscle will relax, and one can increase the stretch by a small amount; stretching on the out breath will considerably improve your technique.

Always be sensitive and aware of your own body as you stretch, as lack of concentration can lead to injury. Do not attempt stretching exercises without instruction; preferably a qualified instructor should be present, as books can be misleading, even if written in great detail. The spine and neck are particularly vulnerable to overstretching through bad technique. You must learn to understand your body and read the warning signs that tell you when your limit has been reached.

These preparatory exercises, particularly the breathing and stretching, are a complete practice in themselves and form the basis of *hatha yoga.* With these alone you can promote mental and physical health.

Ukemi

Ukemi practice usually follows the warm-up period. Its importance has been discussed in detail (Chapter 3). An *aikidoka* must strive to learn good safe *ukemi* so that he can work well with his partner and be safe from potential injury.

The beginner starts by learning to roll both forwards and backwards from a kneeling position. Unlike a gymnastic roll, which is from head to bottom along the spine, the Aikido roll is from one shoulder to the opposite hip, taking a diagonal line across the back. This way, the head avoids contact with the mat and the spine is also protected.

The secret of good *ukemi* is first to relax, then to project the body forwards, not downwards, across the mat. Do not

Forward *ukemi* from a *kokyu nage* throw by Kitaura Sensei.

collapse like a rag doll, nor remain stiff like a lump of wood. Form the body into a wheel from the tip of the little finger along the outside of the arm, shoulder, back and hip and allow the legs to fold under you.

It takes time to learn to control the body in this manner, but it should be remembered that your partner and your teacher are both concerned that you learn well. No one will push you further or faster than you can safely manage, but in a very short time you may find that you can fling yourself forward, from a height, and roll safely, coming back to your feet.

One of the beneficial side effects of good *ukemi* is the ability to survive falling off a bicycle, for example, or tripping over on a hard surface.

Basic techniques
Basic technique relies on an understanding of footwork and handwork. Correct footwork, in particular, gives correct body movement (*tai-sabaki*), so when observing the demonstration of a new technique it is important to pay attention to this aspect; often only one or two steps are taken, and memorizing the order and direction of these may help to reduce a hopelessly complex manoeuvre to something more comprehensible. Then, having placed the body correctly, the hands must be used skilfully to apply the various throws and pins characteristic of Aikido.

Body movement (*tai-sabaki*) can also be practised as a solo exercise, the following basic movements all being suitable for practice in this way:

- *Tsugiashi* – entering rapidly, keeping the same foot forward and pushing off with the back foot.
- *Irimi* – a deep entering step.
- *Tenkan* – pivoting on the leading foot.
- *Irimi-tenkan* – a combined entering and turning movement.

When the *sensei* demonstrates the techniques he will usually call up one of the more senior students (or occasionally even a beginner) to act as *uke*, whilst the rest of the class sits in *seiza* in a line on the edge of the mat. Once the demonstration is completed, the *sensei* will then signal to the class to practise this technique in pairs.

Before practising, students bow to each other, saying '*Onegaishimas*' (please practise with me), and afterwards they bow again, saying '*Domo*' (thank you).

One partner then acts as *uke* for four successive repetitions before reversing roles. Techniques are applied, alternately left and right sided; this promotes symmetry and balance in both partners, and makes allowances for the many left-handed people in our society. This cooperative style of practice means that no scope for competitiveness arises. The *uke–nage* relationship has been discussed already; here it can be seen how, in practice, that cooperation is actively encouraged.

The *sensei* moves among the students, correcting technique, making use of verbal instruction or demonstration. If he sees a common mistake being repeated, he will stop the class and correct the whole class together. By practising with the students, the *sensei* has an opportunity to assist them, while at the same time he develops his own skills. The *sensei* will be particularly aware of correct attitude when practising, so that no personal problems interfere with good practice. Safety is of prime importance and *ukemi* will be constantly monitored, especially with new students.

During paired practice students are encouraged to partner as many others as possible. Pairing off with favourites is rarely a problem, and the highest ranking seniors are often to be found working with the new students, helping them to learn and being helped to develop their own teaching skills.

Inevitably there is much repetition of techniques, until they become second nature. Indeed, in the good old 'bad old days' of martial arts teaching (some veteran *aikidoka* refer almost wistfully to this relatively obsolete style of practice), a single movement, be it a sword cut or body movement, was repeated hundreds of times in order to engrave it on the student's mind. This style of practice still has its place in the class from time to time, but it is less suited to the Western temperament. The same results, or even better, can be achieved by the useful progression of a theme; a single principle is developed in a series of exercises, ranging from the most basic to the most advanced. Although the number of basic principles in any art is finite and usually small, there may be an infinite variety of expressions of those principles. The contemporary approach teaches the student that the art is ultimately creative and that a sound knowledge of principles is a means to its free expression.

In the class, for example, a single technique may be demonstrated in response to the simplest attack. Thereafter, the same response to a variety of attacks may be shown. Eventually technical variations may be introduced until there is a thorough grasp of the principle.

It should always be borne in mind that Aikido is not just about learning techniques as if from a manual. The *aikidoka* learns to use his body in a special way, making use of *hara*, extension of *ki* and leading control. These more abstract principles are hard to teach and may only develop after a long period of regular practice. The student should try to emulate the *sensei* as closely as possible, observing the position of his hands and feet and the orientation of the body throughout the execution of the technique. Gradually, the movements will feel less awkward. Later still, they will feel natural or 'right'.

Ending the class

The normal duration of a class varies from one to two hours. In the case of a two-hour class there may be a short break, with the second hour being devoted to advanced techniques. Ultimately the style and length of a class will depend on a variety of factors, including the range of experience among the students and whether the club practises little and often, or less often with a longer class. The rhythm and pace of the class will also vary, from a fast aerobic style to a gentle slow pace in order to allow a more studied approach.

Eventually the class will wind down, though. The final exercises will be less aerobic, allowing a gentle stretching of joints and muscles. This is very beneficial to the body, and speeds the recovery from stress and exhaustion caused by extremes of exertion.

A recapitulation of the main points of the class may be given, and questions will be answered. However, it must be realized that martial arts practice is concerned with exercising the mind–body, and not just the intellectual mind. Less emphasis is therefore placed on intellectual understanding. The student must have faith that eventually his body will understand the principles directly, and that too much thought can actually interfere with the learning process. However, there is a place for discussion, and a moderate amount is generally allowed.

Finally the students line up in *seiza* as for the beginning of the class. Everybody bows to the *kamiza*, then to the *sensei*. Messages and notices are announced. The *sensei* then leaves the mat, following the reverse protocol as for entering. Students then usually bow to each other and are free to leave the mat.

If the mat is permanent and fixed, it is usually swept at this point. And if the *dojo* belongs to the club, the students will use this time to dust and clean the *kamiza*, the weapons racks and any other areas that require maintenance, e.g. changing rooms.

THE CORE TECHNIQUES

Modern Aikido is founded on a set of basic techniques, including attacks. These evolved over a long period of time, during which the Founder experimented with his knowledge of other martial arts whilst creating his own unique *budo* and bringing it to its mature form. It is both the first and the last task of the *aikidoka* to study and practise these core techniques. Learning the basics is an obvious prerequisite to more advanced practice, but even the most advanced student and teacher will not neglect them.

The following is a brief outline of the basic attacks and techniques the *aikidoka* should master. It is traditional in most martial arts that Japanese terms are used to denote these; although at first it may seem impossible ever to remember or pronounce their names, repetition over a period of time eventually makes them familiar.

Attacks

In a free fight between two individuals, the attacks used probably involve a great variety of punches, kicks, gouges, scratches, perhaps even biting. However, in common with other *budo* and fighting sports, the number of attacks in Aikido has been limited and formalized. Aikido does include some street-fighting attacks such as a straight punch to the head or body, or gripping the lapel with one hand whilst striking with the other, but most of them have evolved from traditional attacks.

For example, two of the most common blows used in Aikido are directly taken from sword attacks. Using the edge of the hand as if it were a blade, *uke* cuts down vertically to the top of *nage*'s head (*shomen-uchi*) or diagonally to the side of the head (*yokomen-uchi*). Neither of these attacks would be commonly used in a practical situation, unless, perhaps, the attacker was holding a weapon such as a bottle or a blunt instrument; their inclusion in the repertoire of basic attacks is mainly to do with Aikido's historical connection with *kenjutsu*.

Kicks are not often used in Aikido, this again being a matter of tradition. However, on the rare occasions when replies to a kick are practised, it is apparent that the same *tai-sabaki* and throwing techniques are, more or less, applicable.

One of the most commonly used attacks in basic practice is a wrist grab (*katate-tori*), in which *uke* grabs either of *nage*'s wrists with one hand. This action may not seem to be a very effective attack, used alone, but it serves several functions:

- It serves as the first step in a blending exercise in which *nage* learns to be aware of the direction and force of *uke*'s *ki* through direct contact, i.e. wrist to hand.

- It is easier to feel a partner's *ki* when there is contact than when the attack is moving. Learning to harmonize with your partner's movement is the first and most fundamental part of practice (hence *aiki* = harmony of *ki*). When there is space between the two of you, *nage* has only his eyes to judge the speed and direction of the attack. When there is contact *nage* can learn to feel *uke*'s *ki*, to sense the direction and force of his intended movement.

- From a wrist grab *nage* learns blending, balance taking and, finally, the application of an immobilization or projection. He can apply the exact same movements to a *shomen* (vertical head strike) in more advanced practice. By this method – progressing from static holding to dynamic striking – a hierarchy of practice strategies, from basic to advanced, can be established.

- Another more practical use of the wrist grab is evident when one remembers that Aikido is not entirely a reflexive art. It is perfectly acceptable to anticipate an intended aggression and make use of preemptive strategies. *Nage* may feint a strike to *uke*'s head. The effects of this may be that *uke* starts to lose his balance as he swerves to avoid the blow. At the same time he may grab *nage*'s wrist to restrain the attack. *Nage* is now in a position to pursue a strategy based on the wrist-grab attack.

To give you an idea of the different types of attack, here is an abbreviated list, giving their Japanese names. This list is not exhaustive; however, there are probably no more than twice as many commonly used attacks as those given here:

- *Katate-tori*, wrist grab – one hand on one wrist, in either the same stance (right to right = *ai-hanmi*) or the opposite stance (right to left = *gyaku-hanmi*).
- *Morote-tori*, two hands grabbing one wrist.
- *Ryote-tori*, two hands grabbing both wrists.

- *Kata-tori,* one hand grabbing the *gi* at the shoulder.
- *Ushiro ryo-kata tori,* grabbing both shoulders from behind.
- *Ushiro ryote tori,* grabbing both wrists from behind.
- *Shomen-uchi,* a straight vertical cutting blow to the head with the hand 'blade'.
- *Yokomen-uchi,* a diagonal cutting blow to the head with the hand 'blade'.
- *Tsuki,* a straight punch, which may be: *jodan* = to the head; *chudan* = to the chest; *gedan* = to the belly.

The techniques – immobilizations and projections

Aikido techniques fall into one of two categories, being either projections or immobilizations. It is not within the scope of this book to describe or teach techniques, so only an outline description can be given.

These *immobilizations* are pinning and holding strategies that restrain further movement by *uke.* The beauty of these applications is that, if correctly applied, *uke* only

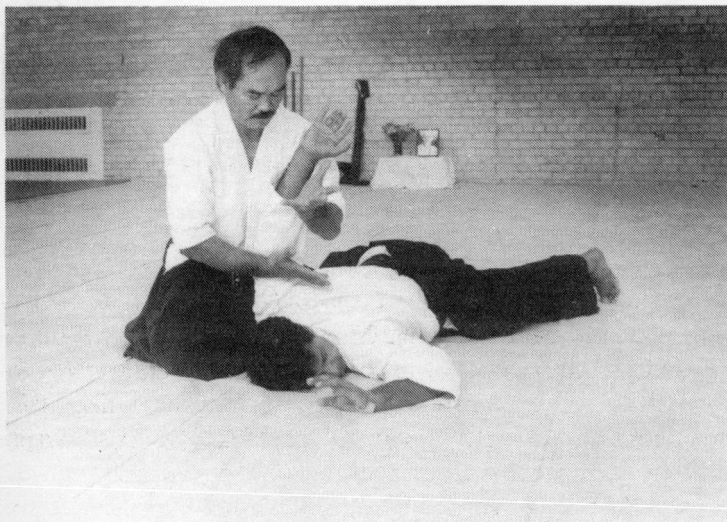

Nikkyo immobilization, locking the shoulder joint.

suffers pain if he resists the movement or tries to struggle once held. The direction of application of the locks is in the direction in which the joints naturally move and not against that movement.

The long-term effects of the locks against the joint commonly used in some martial arts may lead to permanent derangement and damage to the joint, arthritis being a possible consequence of this style of practice. In contrast, the immobilizations used in Aikido may actually improve the health of the joint by stretching the surrounding soft-tissue structures, removing adhesions and increasing the local blood supply. For example, many of the pins involve the shoulder area, which is prone to stiffness as a result of mental stress, neck and shoulder muscles in particular becoming chronically stiff. Regular stretching of the shoulder area reverses this trend, and assists in unlocking and dissipating the stress.

On the mat *uke* learns to trust *nage* by accepting the immobilization as it is being applied. He allows his shoulder to be firmly but gently stretched, and only taps the mat (a universal signal, indicating 'enough') when he feels the comfortable limit of the joint range to be reached. Therapeutic soft-tissue stretching as used by physiotherapists and other 'body workers' is often no more than this. So, one of the lesser known benefits of Aikido practice is its physical therapeutic value.

One group of immobilizations follow from a single principle known as *ikkyo* (meaning 'first'). Following the same nomenclature, the rest are known as *nikkyo* (second), *sankyo* (third), *yonkyo* (fourth), *gokkyo* (fifth) and *rokkyo* (sixth). *Ikkyo* makes use of *uke*'s arm as if it were a crank. Manipulating the arm with a rotary motion focused at the elbow, the whole body is controlled as successive joints become 'locked up'. Combining this cranking motion with a variety of locks to *uke*'s wrist produces the other members of the *ikkyo* group.

An alternative strategy to the immobilization of an attacker is the throw or *projection*. This response comes into its own where there is a multiple attack, for it is then

Kotegaeshi – wrist throw.

clearly impractical, and in fact dangerous, to attempt to pin one attacker whilst another or others are still threatening. In addition to this practical point, throwing techniques are a central and solid part of the traditional origins of Aikido, which include *jujutsu* and *aikijutsu.*

Students must learn the technical aspects of each throw. More fundamentally, they must learn how to stay balanced whilst leading *uke*'s energy in the typical circular and spiral movements that culminate in a throw. Imagine a small object being thrown into a revolving drum and being spun out like a stone from a sling-shot. If the axis of the drum is not balanced and central, the drum itself will be toppled by its own rotational asymmetry. *Aikidoka* therefore spend much of their practice learning to master this gyroscopic principle.

Kokyu nage (literally = breath throw) is the Japanese term given to a series of projections that are not techniques in themselves but are exercises demonstrating basic principles (see Chapter 3). They consist of responses to an attack in which *nage* leads *uke*'s attacking force, unbalancing him in the process, and finally employing *kokyu* (breath power) to send him flying. It is a cooperative exercise, in which *uke* learns to follows *nage*'s movement and consequently loses his balance. However, he learns to regain it once more through the principle of *ukemi. Kokyu nage*, then, prepares both *uke* and *nage* for *waza* (technique) training.

In order to give an idea of the types of throws employed in Aikido, a much abbreviated list has been given below (*nage*, used in the context below, means throw). You should refer to other books on the subject for technical descriptions of how to carry out the techniques. However, I strongly suggest that the only way to learn Aikido is with a qualified instructor; 'how to' manuals in martial arts are, at best, a reminder to already practising students, and, at worst, a dangerous waste of time.

- *Shiho nage*, known as the four-direction throw – makes use of sword *tai-sabaki.*
- *Tenchi nage*, known as the heaven-and-earth throw.
- *Irimi nage*, means entering throw. It is also known as the 20-year technique, owing to its difficulty.
- *Kotegaeshi* – *uke*'s hand is turned outwards at the wrist, compelling the rest of the body to follow suit.

If you consider that there are about 15 basic attacks and a similar number of techniques, each of which can be carried out by entering (*irimi*) or turning (*tenkan*), a minimum of 450 basic techniques emerge (i.e. $15 \times 15 \times 2$). Multiplying this number by two or three, to allow for variations and including the lesser-known techniques, one has the possibility of a thousand or more techniques. Of course the experienced *aikidoka* employs these strategies, not on the basis of memory – an impossible feat – but by demonstrating an unerring knowledge of a few basic principles.

5
ADVANCED PRACTICE

> In Aikido training the ultimate goal is *ki*-mind-body unity.
>
> Kisshomaru Ueshiba

When contemplating taking up a new activity involving skill, what motivates most of us is a vision of the future in which we are masters of the art; we imagine ourselves as adepts, easily performing the most advanced techniques of our latest endeavour. Of course, we don't delude ourselves by thinking that this level of mastery will not be hard won; all the same, we believe we can scale the heights, and finally the ultimate goal is within sight. Now we think of ourselves as experts, and are recognized as such by our peers; we have arrived at our destination, our goal.

Some people give up at this point. A significant proportion of students of martial arts give up when they are awarded *shodan* (first level black belt). Never mind that *shodan* is just the mark of the serious beginner, signifying that a certain understanding of basics has been achieved, and only now can the initiate begin to explore the art in depth and perhaps begin to concentrate more on practising the advanced techniques. However, the unconscious belief that advancement necessarily means moving on from basic practice to advanced technique is erroneous and fails to explain the picture of a great master swordsman practising the same single cut, not a hundred times, but a thousand times; not just for one day, but perhaps every day until his death. Clearly a completely different understanding of the notion and purpose of practice must be held by the serious student of *budo*, when compared to the ideas of our Western achievement-orientated society. This difference may be difficult to grasp for the non-student and beginner; but it lies at the heart of Aikido philosophy, and therefore is worthy of repeated scrutiny.

Let us return to our master of the sword. Is he preparing for a demonstration, a competition, or an exam? Is this cut part of a more intricate series of movements, which he must at some point perform? Perhaps he has mastered the rest of the sequence but lacks finesse in this one movement; once he has perfected it he can move on to a demonstration of the whole sequence, like an ice skater working on a triple spin before incorporating it into the final choreography.

In fact none of these descriptions is accurate. He is not preparing for anything. At the risk of offending those who believe that this life is merely a preparation for the hereafter, I would say that the daily practice of a single sword cut is no more a preparation for a future event than this life, led from day to day, is merely a rehearsal for some other existence. This is your life. Its purpose is intrinsic. The swordsman is not a woodcutter cutting wood to light a fire. The cut is the fire.

Suffice it to say here that advanced practice in Aikido is not a step onward from basic practice, although, of course, advanced practice cannot be considered without a thorough grounding in basics. I suggest, for an answer to this apparent paradox, that we move on from philosophical discussion to the mat.

The following are the areas of advanced practice that will be described in some detail:

- *Suwari-waza*, kneeling techniques (*tachi-waza* means standing techniques).
- *Tantodori*, defence against a knife attack.
- Defence against multiple attacks.
- The elaboration of single movements, practised perhaps initially as exercises, to a stage of greater 'realism' and force.

SUWARI-WAZA

The Japanese traditionally spend a great deal of time on their knees, although perhaps less so today with the influence of Western culture and seating arrangements. However, a typical Japanese room of the traditional style would consist of a *tatami* floor, made from rice straw or rush matting, a fold-away mattress (*futon*) to allow a sleeping room to be converted to a living room, a low table and little else. Those entering the room would first remove their footwear. Then, stepping up on to a platform and through a sliding paper screen (*shoji* screen) that acts as a door, would thereafter proceed on their knees. The peculiar ambulatory form employed by the Japanese in this context was not a stumbling, awkward, shuffling motion, but a graceful and brisk movement that could be carried out in any direction to get the individual to his destination in the room. Having arrived at his destination, the individual would then remain seated in a kneeling

Uke is attacking with *shomen uchi* (vertical head strike). *Nage* preempts the attack, controlling the elbow, prior to completing the immobilization.

position whilst eating, reading, or continuing any other static activity.

For the *samurai* this customary kneeling position posed the problem of security and self-defence, as it was obviously a disadvantageous position. He would of course remain armed, at the least with a short sword. In the position of *seiza* the *samurai* might conceivably expect a sudden attack by another person in the room, also sitting in *seiza.* Or perhaps someone would suddenly burst into the room, mounting an attack from a standing position. *Suwari-waza* (literally sitting technique), is the general term for techniques carried out against an attacker when both are seated in seiza. If the attacker is standing and the defender is seated, these techniques are known as *hanmi-handachi.*

Suwari-waza, then, has its origins in a very practical need for self-defence in what was, in those days, a common situation. The fact that this tradition has been maintained in modern Aikido adds a valuable and unique dimension to its practice. Indeed, O Sensei considered *suwari-waza* to be fundamental to Aikido, and for this reason it is taught early on to beginners and is not strictly speaking advanced.

But for Westerners, who rarely spend any length of time sitting in *seiza* or having to move in a coordinated way on their knees, it appears to be a complicated, awkward and uncomfortable experience. For many who have given up kneeling since early childhood, especially men, the knees, hips and ankles have lost the flexibility to adopt a *seiza* position without considerable discomfort. Also, the muscles required to support the body and allow it to move in this position, particularly the abdominals, back muscles and flexors of the hips, are underdeveloped.

A certain amount of discomfort is therefore inevitable when commencing to practise *suwari-waza*, but in most cases the right degree of flexibility and musculature is eventually achieved. Adequate preparation, involving, for instance, warming-up the joints and muscles, and sensitivity and common sense – not practising 'through' injury

– is always required if the desired end is to be achieved. *Aikidoka* are encouraged to accept and overcome a certain amount of discomfort in their training, and yet to recognize the signs of possible strain or injury and thereby preempt and avoid them. But there is generally a muted sigh of relief when *suwari-waza* ends and students are allowed to stand.

All of the basic techniques of Aikido and many of the more advanced ones can be practised as either *tachi-waza* or *suwari-waza*. *Suwari-waza* builds the *hara*. Because of the altered biomechanics in the kneeling position, balance is affected. When standing, it is easy enough to take a quick step to regain balance if you begin to fall in any direction, but in a kneeling position you may easily fall if you overreach yourself or use too much upper body force in the technique. In *suwari-waza* one learns to feel one's *ki* projecting from the *hara* down to earth to stabilize and balance the upper body, and up and out, through the upper limbs, to execute the technique. In this way *suwari-*

Uke is being thrown with a *shiho nage* projection.

waza greatly affects and improves *tachi-waza*; it has, therefore, more than just traditional or novelty value.

Students of Aikido are first taught how to sit in *seiza*, with the back straight, shoulders relaxed, sitting on the heels, which are together. Then they learn to move on the knees (this activity is called *shikko*). The same *tai-sabaki* (footwork) for standing is also employed in kneeling; so in *shikko* one learns *irimi* (stepping forwards and backwards) and *tenkan* (pivoting on the leading knee). Very soon one learns to move rapidly across the mat in any desired direction.

Disarming *uke* from a knife attack with a choke hold to the throat and a lock on the arm.

Partner practice consists of more or less the same techniques as for standing (they are also given the same names), which may be practised for at least some part of every class.

TANTODORI

Aikido is a classical form of *budo*, as evidenced by the strong connection with sword arts. The principal moving attack is *shomen-uchi*, a vertical strike to the head with the edge of the hand ('hand-blade'). Yet for all its classical style and form, it is eminently practical as a form of self-defence. This is never more apparent than in the practice of *tantodori*, defence against a knife attack.

The *tanto* is a wooden replica of a long-bladed knife, which can be used for stabbing or slashing. Obviously students must be taught the most efficacious ways to attack with the knife and the vulnerable points of the body, and attacks must be realistic to be of any value. However, for beginners they may be slowed down to allow the techniques to be learned in a safe way.

Most of the effective strategies of defence against a knife attack are based on empty-handed attacks, with occasional modifications. The two most obvious modifications that must be learned are, first, changes of grip or other body contact to avoid the risk of being cut whilst dealing with the attack. And second, having brought *uke* to the point of immobilization, the pin may be varied so that *nage* can avoid being cut by the blade and, finally, can compel *uke* to drop the *tanto*. However, these are technical modifications that, in a non-technical book, need not bother you at this stage: but the principles of Aikido – blending, leading control, etc. – do not vary in this special case.

Tantodori teaches you that, although the *tanto*, held in the hand of *uke*, has an almost overwhelming attraction for *nage*, to focus on it is 'fatal'. Weapons are not dangerous, only the people who use them. The practical consequence of this astute caution is the overriding necessity to dominate, and not be dominated by, the source of the attack – *uke's* centre. *Tantodori* is a test of our understanding of basic Aikido principles, for it is when we feel most threatened that we are likely to revert to primitive fear-motivated responses to an attack. Aikido practised diligently and regularly over a long period of time may eventually become ingrained in our bodies and psyches and thereby replace these primitive responses. Thankfully, few of us will need to test this in a truly threatening situation.

MULTIPLE ATTACKS

As you move up through the ranks of Aikido you are expected to be able to show mastery of a defence against two or more attackers. In a grading exam, you may be subjected to a two-person attack, and this may be increased to three or four attackers for more senior gradings. Theory has it that more than four attackers will only impede each other, so if you can handle four you should be able to handle an unlimited number.

The first principle that must be learned in multiple attacks is *tai-sabaki* (body movement), for there is no time to complete sophisticated immobilizations or even elaborate throws. You must learn to move fast and be continually turning, so that your back is not left unprotected. The innovation of the *tai-sabaki* principle *irimi-tenkan* is ideally suited for this purpose (see page 36). A group of attackers will inevitably exhibit a rhythm or pulse as they attempt to overwhelm you; they will be aware of each other as well as of you; and perhaps each will be hoping and waiting for one of the others to take the lead in the attack. *Nage* must be totally open and sensitive to this rhythm. He must enter into a vacuum with a forceful *irimi*, spin energetically with a *tenkan* motion, throwing off attacks from the rear. He must move through the group, sowing chaos in his path, causing the attackers to collide with each other, avoiding their onslaughts with an almost uncanny sixth sense. It is no wonder that this type of practice is of the most advanced kind. To be honest there are few *aikidoka* who can maintain it for more than a few seconds without mishap.

O Sensei used to demonstrate his abilities against multiple unarmed and armed attacks. It is said that he was almost superhuman in his ability to sense and preempt the movements of his attackers. He was able to deal with these attacks with an apparent sense of ease. The *ukes* were left bewildered and confused, and may have wondered how they all had ended up in a heap on the mat.

FROM EXERCISE TO TECHNIQUE

A great percentage of the time spent on the mat involves the practice of exercises, which are, in a sense, conditioning and preparation for the execution and practice of *waza* (technique). Beginning with breathing exercises to focus the mind and relax the body, students move on to stretching and moving exercises. They may then practise *ukemi* (rolling and falling), *tai-sabaki* (foot movements) and *kokyu nage* (breath-throw exercises). Without this preparation *aikidoka* may engage in faulty technique, or may be unprepared physically and mentally for a throw or a pin. The first years of practice therefore essentially consist entirely of preparation (the time scale is vague because it may vary so much with frequency of attendance, age, fitness, etc.). However, if you have taken to heart what has been said so far concerning the purpose of practice, you will understand that this in no way places this length of time of preparation in a secondary or inferior position to the period of time spent in *waza* training.

One of the problems that many beginners have, especially men, is a belief that their techniques must be realistically effective from day one. With this, albeit unconscious, attitude, their movements become stiff and violent, and lack sensitivity. It is quite uncomfortable and often painful to practise with individuals who are in such a state of tension. It is erroneous to believe that because

Aikido is a martial art it should be practised aggressively. I tell my new students, if they have this problem, not to think in terms of overcoming an opponent; instead it is better to think of working with a partner. Learn the movements almost as if learning to dance, and thereby concentrate on balance, fluidity and harmony of movement. Above all, be natural. (I use this analogy of a dance with caution as *budo* is clearly not dance.)

Sometimes beginners are deterred from continuing when they observe a group of senior *aikidoka* apparently being thrown down with great force, to an accompanying resonant hand-slap on the mat (this slapping technique considerably lessens the force of impact). If you are a beginner, you may not realize that there is an immense amount of preparation predating the time when you are able to cope with a forceful throw; nothing is handed out to you that you are not adequately prepared for. *Uke* is able to return to his feet time and again to be thrown a hundred times more; rarely does he sustain more than a mild ache or bruise.

The transition from exercise to technique, from basic to advanced practice, thus involves a continuous and largely unconscious change, which is usually only apparent with hindsight. As you progress along the Way of *aiki*, you are made aware of the famous saying that 'The only thing we have to fear is fear itself'.

Anyone whose primary aim in learning Aikido is self-defence should be aware that, although Aikido is a very practical form of self-defence, it takes many years to achieve the required level of mastery for that purpose. Exercises which may develop *ki* and prepare the *aikidoka* for *waza* (technique) eventually may lead the serious *aikidoka* to a level of expertise suitable for self-defence, but by then the original intention may have long been forgotten. Nevertheless, advanced practice does include realistic and practical responses to full-blooded attacks. The beauty of Aikido is that, having learned *ukemi* to a high level, *nage* is able to practise fully and realistically without holding back. This being the case, the student has a true measure of the efficacy of his technique.

6
WEAPONS PRACTICE

When entering a forest of spears
And they encircle you
Remember, your mind
Is your protective shield

poem, Morihei Ueshiba

The importance of weapons practice in the evolution of
Aikido has already been discussed (see Chapter 2). The
Founder was a master of *bokken* (literally, a wooden
sword) and *jo* (wooden staff), and his knowledge of both
these arts assisted in the formation of Aikido. He
continued to practise and teach *jodo* and *bokken* (there is
no *bokkendo* as such) alongside Aikido until the end of his
days. There is some archive footage, black and white film,
in which the Founder, well into his eighties, is demonstrating *jo-kata*; the *jo* appears to spin around his body
from hand to hand with blurring speed, like the blades of a
helicopter. As a creative master of *budo*, Ueshiba eventually developed his own style of *jo* and *bokken*, and as his
knowledge of weapons grew there was undoubtedly a
cross-fertilization of ideas, strategies, postures and foot
movements that allowed Aikido to come to fruition.
Today, in most *dojo*, *aikidoka* continue to practise *bokken*
and *jo* alongside Aikido. This is partly for the sake of
tradition, but mainly because weapons practice, although
complete in itself, complements the empty-handed art of
Aikido.

Of the two, *bokken* has had by far the greater influence
on Aikido. The very posture (*hanmi*) of Aikido is identical
with that of *bokken*. The *tai-sabaki* is in many cases

76

identical, and some of the techniques of Aikido have their exact counterpart in *bokken* strategies. *Bokken* practice evolved from sword arts, known as *kenjutsu* (literally, sword techniques), which were the quintessential art of the *samurai* (warrior class) of medieval Japan. So supremely lethal were these weapons in the hands of a master that the drawing of a sword invariably signalled the death of one or other of the opponents. For this reason, swords were rarely drawn, and often merely placing a hand on the hilt of a sword would be enough to settle an impending dispute.

The first swords in Japan were made of stone or wood; not until the second century BC was the knowledge available to smelt iron and fashion metal swords. The first recorded single-blade curved sword appears to have been in the Nara period (710–94), but it was the Heian period (794–1185) that saw the advent of what we consider today to be the first definitive Japanese sword. The quality of the sword then continued to improve throughout the Kamakura period (1185–1336), and it is more than mere coincidence that the rise of the *samurai* class ran parallel with this development. The skills of *kenjutsu* were developed throughout the Heian and Kamakura periods, this knowledge becoming systematized in the form of *ryu* (styles) created by individual masters so that, by the Muromachi period (1336–1573), there were hundreds of *ryu*. Partner practice with live blades (i.e. swords sharpened to the keenness of a razor's edge) was far too dangerous, so out of the necessity to pass on the knowledge of sword arts, especially in peacetime, were born the arts of *iaido* and *bokken*.

The first oak *bokken* were used in the early Muromachi period, and over the centuries several hundred *bokken ryu* evolved. Myamoto Mushashi, perhaps the greatest ever Japanese swordsman, is said to have defeated an opponent, Sasaki Kojiro, using a *bokken* against a sword.

Iaijutsu, the defensive art of rapid sword drawing, is traditionally credited to Hojo Jinsuke (sixteenth century), though it is likely to have evolved somewhat earlier. Since the *samurai*, and Japanese in general, sat in *seiza* (kneeling) much of the time, many of the techniques of *iai-jutsu* start from a position of *seiza*. *Iaido* developed during the Meiji period (1868 to the present), the difference between *iaijutsu* and *iaido* reflecting the general trend from *bujutsu* to *budo* (martial techniques to martial Ways) described in Chapter 2.

Kendo was formulated in the late eighteenth century. It is essentially a sport, using bamboo sections to form a straight-bladed sword. Opponents wear light protective armour for the face, head, upper limbs and torso, and points are scored by striking the opponent on certain key areas of the body. Kendo still retains elements of *bujutsu* in its fighting spirit, and elements of *budo* in its discipline and emphasis on mental rectitude. As such, it is regarded by many as an ideal synthesis and an activity of great character-building potential. Perhaps this is why it is taught as part of the curriculum in many Japanese schools.

Today, sword arts still flourish in Japan and throughout other parts of the world as well. And, thanks to Ueshiba, *bokken* practice is an integral part of modern Aikido.

THE *BOKKEN*

The *bokken* is a wooden replica of a Japanese *katana* (sword). It is not an exact replica, as such a narrow blade

The *bokken*.

The *katana*.

made of wood might easily break and would be too light to be of any use. However, the length is approximately the same, and it is curved in a similar manner. The cross section is oval at the handle, the blade being of a variety of shapes.

The best *bokken* are made of Japanese oak, white oak, it is said, being better than red. This wood is strong, heavy and flexible enough not to shatter after repeated impacts. The grain should be straight, with no end grain appearing along the length of the weapon, for if the grain is twisted along its length the *bokken* will warp and lose its intended shape. You can check the straightness of the grain by observing both ends of the weapon to see if the grain lines are parallel, one end with the other. If there is end grain along the length of the *bokken* it will most likely break at this point, splitting along the length of the exposed grain.

You must also choose a wood that is free of knots. The knots mark where branches originally grew out from the stem, and they are usually hard and brittle, such that an impact will not transmit through their substance but instead cause it to shatter.

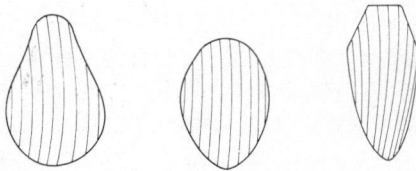

Typical *bokken* cross sections.

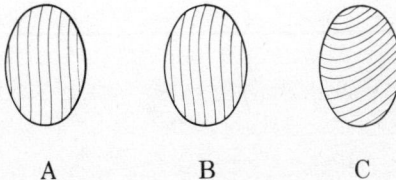

A   B   C

For a *bokken* with a hilt cross section A, B represents a good straight grain, whereas C is twisted relative to A.

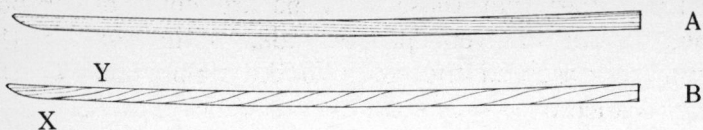

A. Grain is good.
B. A split can occur anywhere along the lines of grain where end grain is exposed, e.g. along line XY.

Close examination of the surface may reveal other abberrations of the wood which, in general, are contra-indications of top quality. Looking along the length of the *bokken*, close one eye and check that the curve is constant and not severe. Only the slightest of curves is necessary, and a steep curve is likely to produce exposed end grain at either or both ends. Preferably the *bokken* should not taper towards the 'point' as this will result in a weaker 'blade', with poor balance. This type of *bokken* is often found in martial arts shops and, unfortunately, in the *dojo*, but is usually of moderate to poor quality. Finally, you should hold the *bokken*; feel its weight and balance; move it; cut with it. For this, you obviously need the assistance of someone with knowledge and experience; learning to choose quality is, in all instances, a matter of careful consideration and experience. Most martial arts shops stock the cheaper or middle range *bokken*; but, while the latter may suit the beginner, for the serious student who wishes to engage in partner practice, I suggest one expensive *bokken* is worth several smashed cheaper varieties (a good quality *bokken* costs about £30 – 1991 prices).

Weapons are kept in a cloth bag, both for their protection and to make them less conspicuous. Once a year it is worth giving them a light rub down with teak oil to preserve the wood. It is also best to keep wooden weapons away from extremes of temperature, and to store them in such a way that they will not warp or bend. In a permanent *dojo* you will often see them stored on a horizontal rack, each supported by two pegs.

Remember that these weapons are not mere implements, toys, or even sporting aids; to the *samurai* the sword represented the soul. To the serious *budoka* the significance of weapons transcends their practical value. Therefore, they should be treated with great respect, and not thrown down or left untidily.

BOKKEN PRACTICE

In some *dojos* there are classes solely for weapons practice; otherwise, a part of each class may be set aside for this purpose. Students are encouraged always to bring weapons to the class in case they are needed.

Bokken practice can be broken down into the following areas:

- Etiquette.
- Grip.
- *Suburi.*
- *Kata.*
- *Awasi.*
- *Tachidori.*

Etiquette

With or without a weapon, *dojo* etiquette does not vary significantly. However, in the former case you must learn, in addition, how to hold and position the weapon whilst entering or leaving the mat, whilst moving about the mat and while making the *rei.* For example, when picking up or putting down a weapon a small *rei* is performed to the weapon in the direction of the *kamiza.* This is done by holding it out in both hands, at arms length, and bowing slightly from the waist.

The details of etiquette will not be described here. What is important for the beginner student to realize is its significance, for all that has been said earlier concerning etiquette also holds for weapons practice. The rules of etiquette should be strictly adhered to; they are, as has been pointed out, a central part of practice. Weapons

Swordsman silhouetted in a doorway in *kamae* posture.

practice can be dangerous if carried out in an unconscious or disrespectful way. Etiquette serves as a reminder to the *aikidoka* to stay ever mindful of the nature of the art he is practising and to take care of his partner's welfare.

The grip
The new student first learns how to hold a *bokken* and how to stand in correct stance (*kamae*).

The two-handed grasp is unlike the Western swordstyle.

The grip is light, yet firm, the handle being pressed into the palms by the fourth and fifth fingers. The third finger applies less pressure and the index finger almost no pressure at all. The fingers are not stiff. Held in this way, the weapon is unlikely to be dropped or knocked from the hands. At the same time the hands will not tire easily. The correct grip gives, in addition, increased sensitivity and awareness of what is happening.

This same grip is also used when holding a partner's wrist, for example in the attack *katate tori*. It is a sticky grip, hard to shake off. Furthermore, with practice, you can also feel not only your partner's slightest movement, but also his level of tension.

The left hand grips the very end of the *bokken*, the right hand is placed about a hand's-width above the left, and the point of the *bokken* is aimed at the level of the throat of the partner. In this position you imagine your *ki* flowing from the *hara*, up through the body, down the arms, along the weapon and out of the tip, like a continuous and unending stream of light, beaming to infinity.

Suburi

The *suburi* are the basic cuts employed in the use of the *bokken*, forming the building blocks from which the art is constructed. There are seven commonly practised *suburi*, these being practised by all levels, from beginner to the most advanced.

It is in the practice of *suburi* that the true essence of Japanese or *zen* type of training is manifested. The same cut may be repeated a thousand times. Several hundred repetitions may be asked for without a break, a small consolation being that after the first hundred repetitions it becomes easier. Whether this is due to the arms becoming anaesthetized by endless repetition I don't know, but I rather suspect it is due to the student having to stop using strength as the muscles become exhausted. It is difficult to endure this type of practice if one is impatient to make progress or achieve some end result, and it may seem tedious or boring to the uninitiated, even though this style of teaching has been modified somewhat in martial arts training in general in order to accommodate Western tastes. However, it should be remembered that students come to martial arts to study, to understand the secrets they may impart, and too much compromise defeats this purpose.

The first *suburi* holds the key to an understanding, not only of the sword, but of Aikido as well. It involves a vertical cut, made straight down through the centre of an imaginary opponent. The left hand, as a general principle, stays on the centre line (a vertical line bisecting the *bokken* holder's body into two symmetrical halves); it is the hand that gives movement and power to the cut. The right hand directs the cut. In the first *suburi*, the left hand raises up and cuts down the centre line, whilst the right hand maintains the *bokken* on a straight vertical line, not allowing it to deviate to the right or left.

This simple *shomen* cut is in turn the basis of many Aikido techniques. It is a matter of principle that *nage*'s hands rarely leave the centre line throughout the execution of a technique. Movements along the centre line are powerful and hard to resist. Deviation from the centre line is biomechanically unsound. The loss of centre is immediately felt as a loss of control of *uke* and your own integrity. To keep the hands and arm movements on the centre line instinctively throughout the execution of a technique can take years to master, but practice of this first *suburi* assists the process of mastery.

The seven *suburi* are well described in volume one of Saito Sensei's comprehensive series on Aikido. They are often practised first in a weapons session, the class usually synchronizing cuts to a count of one to 10 in Japanese (so if he achieves nothing else, the student at least learns to count to 10 in Japanese). *Suburi* practice prepares the *aikidoka* for more advanced partner practice and is a *sine qua non* for the latter. However, that should not be regarded as its sole purpose. As with all 'practice', the idea of any activity being a means to an end is misleading and contrary to the spirit of *budo*.

Kata

If you link together a series of basic movements, including perhaps some or all of the *suburi*, the result is a *kata*. *Kata* exist in most *budo* as a method of practising fundamental movements or exercises in one quick flowing pattern. *Kata* are the basic 'forms' of a martial art. Once memorized, a *kata* can be practised regularly by the group in unison, or at other times as a solo exercise. It is an excellent and enjoyable method of imprinting basic movements into the memory. The main drawback of *kata* practice is the tendency not to execute each movement precisely, and it is also difficult to be aware of errors, which may therefore go uncorrected.

Kata for *bokken* (in the context of Aikido) are rare. In fact I am only aware of one, created by Chiba Sensei. It is an eight-movement *kata* consisting of a pattern of movements varied in eight different ways. It takes perhaps two minutes to perform, and yet it contains within it all the

Chiba Sensei prepares to defend himself against a *shomen-uchi* attack.

85

basic cuts, thrusts and footwork of *bokken* practice.

Awase

Partner practice with *bokken* is formalized in a way similar to Aikido practice, so that students study and repeat a series of stereotyped encounters in which each knows the role he has to perform. However, one major difference with *bokken* is the use of 'counters'. A 'counter' occurs when person A attacks, B executes the technique, A then counters the technique (i.e. avoids B's technique and applies his own), and B may then counter the counter, and so on.

Saito Sensei describes five *awase* in volume one of his series on Aikido and weapons practice. They consist of a series of one-attack, one-reply encounters, designed to teach basic attacking moves. Partners learn good *maai* (fighting distance) and *tai-sabaki* (body movement), while at the same time gaining precision in their cutting and thrusting.

A wooden *bokken* is a potentially lethal weapon. It was not only used for practice in medieval Japan; in fact, there are documented instances in the history of *budo* where the *bokken* has out-fought the sword. Japanese oak will turn a steel blade if the parry is well-executed. For this reason, and because the emphasis has changed from *jutsu* to *do* (see Chapter 2 on history and philosophy), *bokken* practice is not free fighting. For a start, a lifetime could be spent mastering the essential sword movements included in the *suburi* and *awase*. Furthermore, some of the more advanced partner exercises, involving several attacks and counter attacks, require split-second timing and great skill on the part of both protagonists, without any need for one to prove his superiority over the other.

However, Chiba Sensei was aware that formalized partner practice could lead to a loss of understanding of the true nature of the sword. Real-life encounters usually involved a single lethal and decisive reply to an attack; the Errol Flynn cut and thrust style of swordsmanship was not a typical feature of Japanese sword style. Instead the one who walked away, as opposed to being carried away, was he who dominated the other's centre with his own centre; in practice this meant he used his sword to dominate the other's sword. Shihan T.K. Chiba therefore created a series of *bokken* domination exercises to illustrate this concept. These exercises appear to be technically simple, but the reality is far from that, and failure truly to reach out with one's spirit to overcome the other's attack is immediately apparent in the outcome of the exchange.

The knowledge gained from the practice of *bokken* domination can be used in *awase* and partner practice. It brings them to life in a very real way, and answers those critics who may argue that formal practice (literally, the practice of 'forms') lacks realism.

Tachidori

The prime art of the *samurai* was swordsmanship. But what is the *samurai* to do in the event that the sword falls, or is struck from his hands? Perhaps the code of honour or *bushido* might regard this as a shameful event (the separation of a *samurai* from his sword), requiring immediate defeat as a form of atonement. However, this aspect aside, the art of dealing with a sword attack for someone who is or has become disarmed is an interesting and vital part of *tachidori* practice. The techniques that *aikidoka* are taught in order to take away the sword from the swordsman illustrate well the close conceptual and historical alliance of Aikido and sword, for several of the techniques of *tachidori* rely on controlling the attacker by means of locks to the wrist. It is hard for an unarmed person to inflict pain or injury to someone wearing armour (the typical lightweight armour of the *samurai* soldier), but the wrists must be free to move, to function in battle, and this makes them relatively easy targets for a determined opponent. It is therefore likely that the series of wrist-controlling techniques so well-known (sometimes painfully so) to the *aikidoka* grew out of battlefield situations of this nature.

It is natural that if a person spends his life perfecting an art based on one set of principles, he would want to apply those principles to other situations rather than learn a whole new way of responding. Arm, foot and body movements which were so ingrained in the *samurai*'s sword style as to appear instinctive, would therefore naturally be applied to unarmed situations, without the need for forethought. *Tachidori* is thus essentially Aikido practised against a partner armed with a *bokken*.

Aikido was created to deal with any number of attackers, armed or unarmed. There is therefore some irony in the notion of an unarmed *aikidoka* disarming a swordsman, the very art from which Aikido was originally derived.

THE *JO*

The Japanese *jo* is a weapon not unlike the English quarter-staff. The heritage is also similar, in that neither were weapons of the aristocracy or of professional soldiers, but rather were favoured by commoners, wanderers, priests and outlaws. In England this weapon was immortalized by Robin Hood in the legendary fight on a narrow bridge with Little John.

The *jo*.

In the East the forerunner of the *jo* was the *bo* (a staff exceeding 6 feet in length), originating in China and probably brought to Japan by itinerant priests. There were no techniques as such before the sixth century, and the art was not systematized until the Kamakura period (1185–1336) by the *So-hei* warrior priests. Izasu Levov (1387–88) created the first *ryu* for *bo*, called the *katori ryu*.

Myth has it that the first *jo* was created by Muso

Gomosuke. He was a master of *bo* (the *katori ryu*), and was undefeated against allcomers, including swordsmen. One day he met the legendary swordsman Myamoto Mushashi, who defeated him in a duel but who spared his life for his singular bravery and skill. Muso Gomosuke then spent years pondering his defeat and meditating on the reason for it, until a 'divine' cryptic message led him to cut down his *bo* to a shorter length (about 4 feet), creating the first *jo*. He then developed five basic techniques, and, returning to Myamoto Mushashi, defeated him for the first and only time in Mushashi's life, also sparing his life (to return the favour). And so this weapon, though of humble origins, simple design and material, is versatile enough to overcome the supreme weapon of all, the Japanese sword.

Jojutsu developed during the Tokugawa period (1603–1868), where its non-lethal nature made it ideal for practice combat. It became a *do* form in 1955, although still retaining a close likeness to the original *bujutsu* (fighting) form. In its original form, *jojutsu* is usually practised against a sword or *bokken*. In modern Aikido, however, most partner practice involves both partners using a *jo*.

The *jo* itself is a straight staff, about 4 feet in length and of circular cross section. Ideally it is made of Japanese oak for strength, density and flexibility. As with the *bokken*, the wood should be straight-grained and preferably unblemished. A *jo* should be selected and cared for in much the same way as has been already described for the *bokken* (a good quality *jo* costs about £25 - 1997 prices). Make sure you sight along its length; it should be dead straight, and slide through the hands with a frictionless balanced feel.

JO PRACTICE

Etiquette
Apart from some minor technical differences, the etiquette for *jo* practice does not vary significantly from that of *bokken*. The underlying significance is the same, and the

Starting position for *jo* practice.

reader is referred to the corresponding section on *bokken* for an explanation of this (see page 81).

The grip

The *jo* is a uniform weapon without a region that could be described as a handle. In fact the versatility of this weapon stems, in part, from the fact that it can be held anywhere along its length and that either end may serve to deliver a blow to an opponent.

There are however two basic starting positions for most *jo* exercises.

- The *jo* may be held in both hands, one hand at the end of the *jo*, the other about 12 inches forward from the first. The *jo* is then held more or less parallel to the ground, pointing at the opponent.
- Alternatively the *jo* is held vertically by one hand, at arm's length and chest height, with one end supported on the floor.

The *jodoka* stands in a posture similar to Aikido posture, and from either of these two standing positions most *suburi, kata* and paired exercises may commence.

Suburi

Jo suburi consist of straight thrusts, either forwards or backwards, and swinging arc-like blows to the vulnerable areas of the body. It is essential that these individual attacking moves are practised thoroughly before moving on to *kata* and partner practice.

Although the principles of *jo* are not so evident in the practice of Aikido, certain elements of *jo* style have made their contribution; for example, the deep forward-thrusting strike used in *jo*, and, for that matter, bayonet attacks, almost certainly contributed to *irimi* or entering techniques of Aikido.

Kata

Jo practice really comes into its own in the practice of *kata*. The 31-move *kata* described by Saito Sensei (volume one, *Traditional Aikido*) contains a series of basic offensive and defensive movements, linked together to form a graceful and flowing whole. Once memorized (a feat in itself), the *kata* teaches good footwork (*irimi* and *tenkan*), balance and weapon handling, while, in addition, the *jo-doka* learns to move his body in a fluid continuous manner. However, there is danger, if too much emphasis is placed on *kata*, of the practice devolving into a sophisticated style of dance; the individual thrusts, strikes and parries may then lose their significance, become technically incorrect, and be lost in the dance-like complexity of the *kata*. For this reason *kata* should always take second place to basic *suburi* and partner practice.

There are two well-known *kata*; the '31' *kata* by Saito Sensei, and a 13-move *kata*. I have also heard of a 21-move *kata*, and there are surely others. And of course there is no proscription against inventing your own.

Tsuki attack to the chest.

Awase

Most experienced *aikidoka* are aware of the existence, even if they haven't read them, of the series of hard-backed texts by Saito Sensei, that cover all the basics and some of the more advanced practice of Aikido and weapons. *Bokken* and *jo* practice are outlined in detail in one or more volumes and the majority of *dojos* of the various schools commonly use these sources as a syllabus for weapons practice. One of Saito Sensei's greatest contributions to Aikido (apart from being one of the most senior and respected *senseis*) was the precision and accuracy with which he observed and recorded Ueshiba's teachings. His Aikido series is, then, an invaluable permanent record of those teachings, as seen through the eyes of a most senior master of the art.

There are those in the Aikido community who have argued that weapons practice should consist of trying one's best to emulate the teachings as recorded by Saito Sensei, so that a kind of orthodoxy has thereby been established. Certainly the *aikidoka* has nothing to lose, and a great deal to gain, by spending a lifetime studying and practising according to these texts (under the guidance of a qualified instructor). Two considerations should, however, be borne in mind. First, Aikido is an art as well as a discipline. As an art it is subject to the creative process and, therefore, inevitably, to change. Secondly, no matter how accurately someone appears to observe and record a series of events, the recording will always be subject to and affected by the interpretation of the recorder – the well-known 'observer effect'. This may seem like heresy to some – the idea of Aikido as a living art that continues to grow and change. But is it not even possible that Ueshiba, had he lived longer, might have continued to develop and change his teachings? My teacher once said to me that the form of Aikido that we practise is not the important thing: rather, we should remain true to the *spirit* of Aikido and the Founder.

But why this talk of orthodoxy in a section on *jo* partner practice? For many years I practised 'orthodox' *jo* style, and benefited greatly from the teachings. Saito Sensei's style laid the cornerstone of my own practice. Wherever I visited and practised Aikido, and particularly *jo*, I found this style not very different from that which was being taught at each *dojo*.

Then I began to study under Shihan T.K. Chiba, whom I believe to be among the foremost proponents of weapons arts among the Aikido *shihan*. What he appeared to be teaching with respect to *jo* seemed somewhat different to that which I had previously learned. Technically it appeared more dynamic. Thrusting attacks had greater depth of penetration, the *jo* corkscrewing forwards to challenge the partner's centre. But what struck me most about what I was learning was that it could be 'dangerous'. It required a positive response – good *ukemi* – to avoid being struck (usually on the knuckles). It was a case of having to learn or suffer the painful consequences; learning to receive an attack became as important, if not more so, than learning to deliver one. What had been a formal art for me thus acquired a little of the 'living on the

Taking *ukemi* from a *jo* strike.

edge' taste that the old-fashioned *jutsu* styles of weapons training must have had in their heyday.

Over a period of two years, and I believe as the culmination of many years of concentrated study, Chiba Sensei developed a set of 36 exercises for partner practice, consisting of sets of 12 replies to each of the following:

- A *yokomen* attack – a swinging cut to the side of the head.
- A *shomen* attack – a vertical blow to the head.
- A *tsuki* attack – a straight thrust to the body.

Since these are the three most common and basic attacks in *jo* training, the 12 replies to each offer a comprehensive repertoire for the *jodoka*. They will, I am sure, form the foundation of a *jo* style that will develop and grow from strength to strength; and will serve to remind us that we are practising a creative art, and that change in itself is not something to fear.

IAIDO

Iaido is the -*do* form of *iaijutsu,* the defensive art of quickly drawing the sword and slaying an attacker. *Iaido* is performed alone, the attacker being imaginary. Even so, the response to an imagined attack is executed with precision.

The practice of *iaido* is quite separate and independent from Aikido. However, they have much in common, principally their meditative approach and the common use of sword principles. Perhaps for these reasons a certain number of *aikidoka* practise both. In addition, a small number of Aikido teachers also teach *iaido.*

Iaido is practised with a sword, which may have a live blade (*katana*) or be an alloy copy (*iaito*), the latter being lighter, much cheaper and blunt. This bluntness is no small consideration; practising with a live blade requires great concentration and precision, not only for the sake of good practice, but also for the sake of retaining the requisite number of fingers!

In *iaido* the student responds to an imaginary opponent. Great emphasis is placed on close attention to precise details in every aspect of training: how the *katana* is picked up, held and placed in the belt; the correct behaviour at the beginning and end of a practice session; and, of course, the techniques themselves. The student learns to draw the sword from its scabbard, step and cut or thrust, remove the 'blood' from the blade with a single movement and then sheath the sword. The *iaidoka* begins in a balanced, silent, concentrated repose, and returns to the same state, the whole movement from start to finish having a symmetry, grace and apparent ease – the result of many hours of concentrated practice.

7
ORGANIZATION
AND
HIERARCHY

Aikido is not an art for defeating others. It is for the unification of the world and the gathering together of all races into one family.

Morihei Ueshiba

The popularity of Aikido continues to increase steadily, so that, at the time of writing, it is practised by more than a million people worldwide. It cannot claim to match the greater participation in judo, partly because it is not a competitive sport (judo has been an Olympic event since 1964) offering public spectacle and the incentive of trophy-winning. Nevertheless its attractions are slowly becoming recognized by a wider spectrum of the population.

Martial arts tend to attract young athletic men more than any other sector of society and the less robust are often put off by their image of physical excess and potential violence. In many cases this image is unfounded and never more so than in the practice of Aikido.

My own observation and participation with a wide variety of groups throughout the world, led me to the conclusion that Aikido is suitable for allcomers who are medically fit. I am no longer surprised at the high percentage of high-ranking women students and teachers. Nor is it a rarity to find elderly enthusiasts, of a frail disposition, practising gently within the group.

Children are also often to be found practising with

adults on courses. One area which does require greater development is that of children's classes. Generally it is better that children practise within their own special group so that their particular needs may be catered for. On the occasions that I have practised with children it has been great fun; but more than that, I have learned a great deal from the natural and relaxed way in which they use their bodies. The psychological blocks and defences which often manifest themselves in later life, in stiff, ungainly and self-conscious movement, have not yet had time to form. And with luck and perhaps the continued practice of Aikido they may never do so.

ORGANIZATION

Although today there are many organizations using the word Aikido in their titles, it should be remembered that this discipline was the creation of one man and that the many groups currently practising sprang initially from one *dojo*. This *dojo*, known as Kobukan, opened in 1931 in

Tokyo. It was a single-storey wooden building where Morihei Ueshiba held his classes. A new *dojo* was built on the same site as the old in 1967, this being a five-storey building accommodating 600 students and employing 30 full-time *shihan* (senior masters). It is called Hombu *Dojo* and is the world Aikido headquarters. When O Sensei died in 1969 his son Kishommaru Ueshiba became the head of the Aikikai – the name given to this organization when it was formed in 1945.

Traditionally, martial arts were considered to be secret arts, only to be passed on to specially selected individuals. To enter Hombu in the early days therefore required that individuals be rigorously interviewed and tested to ascertain their worthiness. With the new spirit of *aiki*, a product of O Sensei's deeply held religious and spiritual beliefs, came the notion that Aikido should be available to everyone. Of course people with a violent nature, wishing to abuse its secrets, would be banned from practice, but, initially, any individual genuinely seeking the knowledge should be given a chance to commence practice. It is due to Kishommaru Ueshiba's vision and hard work that the spread of Aikido outside Japan has been so successful. While his father was alive, the job fell to him of organizing and sending *shihan* abroad to set up and teach new groups, which then became satellite members of the Aikikai.

The first such visit to the West was made by Tadashi Abbe Sensei, a former *uchideshi* of O Sensei. He arrived in France in 1953 and began teaching there. He also visited other European countries, introducing Aikido and giving instruction. Thirty countries attended the first International Aikido Federation Conference held in Madrid in 1975, and by 1984 there were 40 member countries. At this time Hombu *Dojo* was only prepared to recognize one organization in each country; the *shihan* would be appointed by Hombu *Dojo* and would act as principal and technical director for all the member *dojos* of that country, thus ensuring the maintenance of standards and style, and allowing Hombu *Dojo* to exercise ultimate control. Considerations such as the determination of rank, gradings and syllabus would be the responsibility of Hombu *Dojo*.

This intention, of having a *shihan* based in each member country, who would be the head of each respective national Akikai, was based on the idea of an organization spreading upwards and outwards from a single seed, with all its members connected, like the branches of a tree connected to the main trunk. However, human nature being what it is, this ideal has not so far been realized, and the current situation is far more complex. Continuing the analogy of a tree, seeds were shed early on which have gone on to produce separate growths of their own; most of these are 'hybrids' and one or two appear to be of a different 'species' altogether, it being debatable whether they warrant the title 'Aikido' at all.

Perhaps it was a vain hope that each generation of followers of O Sensei should wish to practise Aikido exactly as he did. As was pointed out earlier, Aikido is a creative art that inevitably changes with time and with the individual. O Sensei, had he lived another 20 years, would probably be practising something considerably different from the Aikido he taught in the late 1960s before his death. And O Sensei's students, some of whom went on to become senior masters, placed their own interpretation and bias on his teachings.

Although the Aikikai is still the major organization for the promotion of Aikido, there are now others that have international standing. The three most notable of these are: Aikido Yoshinkai, the Ki Society, and the Tomiki School.

Aikido Yoshinkai
This is the second largest international organization after the Aikikai. It follows the teachings of Shihan Gozo Shioda. Shioda Sensei studied with O Sensei, predominantly during the prewar (Second World War) period. Yoshinkai Aikido very much reflects the Founder's earlier 'harder' style. It is generally considered to be less flowing, and less circular, with a greater emphasis on practical self-defence aspects.

The Ki Society

Shihan Koichi Tohei was on of O Sensei's most senior ranking and highly respected disciples. He placed great emphasis on the nature and development of *ki*, and considered exercises to enhance and test one's *ki* to be a cornerstone of Aikido practice. Tohei Sensei went on to form the Ki Society, and Ki Aikido is now practised in many countries throughout the world, notably in the USA and to a lesser extent in Great Britain.

The Tomiki School

Another senior *shihan* to break away from the Aikikai was Tomiki Sensei. He was, prior to his Aikido training, a master of judo, and saw in Aikido the possibilities of a sporting style that might suit younger members of the community wishing to compete. He envisaged a style of Aikido, along with judo and kendo, as a major character-building activity and even part of the Japanese school curriculum.

Tomiki Aikido is also practised throughout the world; in Great Britain it is principally represented by the British Aikido Association (BAA–see page 112 for addresses). However, it is not traditional Aikido, having foresworn the basic precepts of traditional *budo* in favour of competitive sporting principles. It has undergone a metamorphosis similar to that which judo underwent as it changed from *jujutsu*. Many of the techniques are now barely recognizable as traditional techniques, for they have to be modified and attacks changed to fit in with a point-scoring system and to allow competition to take place meaningfully and safely.

The above are all examples of international organizations that have long since established their independence from the Aikikai. There are, however, other organizations at a strictly national level that have been formed for a variety of reasons, Great Britain containing some examples of these. The current *shihan* (since 1977), principal and technical director of the British Aikido Federation (BAF, until recently the only official branch of the Aikikai in this country) is Kanetsuka Sensei. He took over this position from Chiba sensei, who then returned to Japan before settling in California as the head of the Western USA Federation. Inline with Hombu policy, the BAF was the soleofficialbody representing the Aikikai in this country, with the Ki Society and the BAA (representing Tomiki style) existing independently. The British Aikido Board was formed by a small number of Aikido associations in 1975 and has since grown to represent the majority of groups practising Aikido in the country today. Membership is open to all associations irrespective of 'style'. The BAB is recognised by the Sports Council as the governing body for Aikido in the United Kingdom and is represented on the Sports Council Advisory Group on Martial Arts.

The BAB Coaching Award Scheme is recognised nationally and ensures that Aikido instructors have the necessary skill and expertise to teach others. Candidates are only allowed to attend training courses if their Associations have vetted their basic skills. Moreover, to hold any of the Board's Coaching Awards instructors must have undertaken appropriate First Aid training and maintained it at regular intervals (at least every 3 years).

The three major groups – BAF, UKA and BAB – all practise a similar, traditional style of Aikido and, although independent of each other, they are all connected to the source of Aikido via their respective *shihan*. In this way they can continue to absorb 'nourishment' and grow in the Way of *aiki*. No doubt they will change as they develop; their respective *shihan* have their individual styles, which inevitably leave their mark. Of greater concern are the smaller isolated groups, which have ceased to look to a higher authority for their sustenance. The danger here is that, like a limb separated from the tree, they will wither and die out, or become unrecognisable as forms of Aikido. Still, there is nothing to be done about this; individuals be free to choose their own path in this world. However, it is hoped by progressively minded students and teachers of Aikido that eventually these independent organizations will form a federation of federations. It is not expected, nor even desirable, that they should lose their autonomy; it is undoubtedly healthier for Aikido as a whole that they should continue to flourish, and grow in their own ways. But it would be of great common interest if they were to form an association of equal partners, to allow the cross-flow of ideas, teachers and common aims. This state of affairs is for the future, though, since it certainly does not exist today.

As a prospective beginner you should investigate your local area to see what choices are available; you can perhaps write to the head offices of the organizations listed on page 111 to see if a *dojo* of that affiliation exists locally. Then you should go along and observe or practise without commitment. If you are concerned about the organization to which the particular *dojo* is affiliated, ask questions, but remember that some are independent. In the larger towns and cities there is often a choice of *dojos*, but in the provinces there may be only one possibility, and that may lie at some distance. Aikido is becoming more widespread each year, which undoubtedly is a good thing; however, with its increasing popularity grows the danger that standards of teaching may fall. This last factor is perhaps one of the best reasons why a *dojo* affiliated to an official organization should be sought.

After a trial period, students are generally expected to become members of their chosen *dojo*. An annual fee of about £25 (1997 prices) is normally required for membership, by the parent organization. This figure will include third party liability insurance. Since no insurance company will insure an individual privately for anything like this price, it is a real bargain. If your *dojo* is not affiliated to a major organization it is advisable to discuss the question of insurance with your *sensei*.

Mat fees may be paid on the night, monthly or annually, depending on the *dojo*. Prices are, on average, £4.00 a session (1997 prices), though there are some commercial *dojos* which charge a lot more. Unless the *sensei* needs to live by his teaching, devoting the majority of his time to this endeavour, I suggest you regard high-priced, commercial *dojos* with some suspicion.

RANK AND GRADING

Rank in Aikido is measured in a manner similar to that devised by Jigoro Kano (the founder) for judo – the *kyu / dan* system. Students are initially without rank. After a prescribed number of hours of teaching they are eligible to take an exam for sixth *kyu*. After a further period of training they are examined for fifth *kyu*. This process continues up to first *kyu*, the time interval between gradings increasing geometrically. In some *dojos* coloured belts denoting *kyu* rank are worn, but in the main all *kyu* grades wear white belts.

After a minimum of one year's practice a first *kyu* student may examine for *shodan* (first degree black belt). Then, two years after *shodan*, they may test for *nidan* (second degree black belt). The *dan* grade system is thus in ascending order, from first to tenth degree.

The Founder and his son (known as Doshu) are outside the ranking system. The *shihan* are the senior masters of Aikido, and vary in rank, usually from sixth *dan* upwards. In general, though, you will be expected to have achieved a minimum of *shodan* level before going on to teach. Even so, you must never fall into the trap of believing yourself to be no longer a student. To lose sight of one's 'beginner's mind' is disastrous, and may signal the end of true practice.

Gradings take the form of a demonstration by the student. A period of time is usually set aside for this purpose during a course led by a senior instructor. As a student you should not be in a hurry to take exams. It is better to wait until you are completely prepared so you are not pushed beyond your level of ability. Nevertheless, being watched and assessed in front of a large group of seniors and peers is always a nerve-racking experience. The grading exam considered in this light is a demonstration of technical ability and a test of character with no competitive element either apparent or implied.

This grading system was introduced partly to satisfy the needs of students who required some feedback concerning their progress, although strictly speaking this concept of progress is inconsistent with the fundamental principles of Aikido. There is a familiar story amongst *aikidoka* of a student who asked his *sensei* how long it would take him to achieve *shodan*. 'Ten years' replied the *sensei*. 'And if I practise twice as hard as I am doing now?' asked the student. 'In that case it will take 20 years', concluded the *sensei*. The moral of this story is that too much emphasis on achieving results, getting on, making progress, is ultimately self-defeating; practise for today and let tomorrow's practise take care of itself. Notwithstanding that advice, gradings do have their place; they are good tests of character and, eventually, are important for the would-be teacher of Aikido.

It is theoretically possible to achieve *shodan* in three years, but there are those who have practised 10 years or more and remain *kyu* grade. There is no pressure, from any quarter, for individuals to take exams. The opportunity is always there; but the decision is ultimately a free one. Personal advancement, however it is measured, was undoubtedly of secondary importance to the Founder of Aikido. His aims lay far above the cultivation of the ego. Love of all sentient beings and world peace lie at the heart of his teaching. He believed this could be achieved through the daily battle to conquer the spirit; through the practice of true *budo* – Aikido.

APPENDIX:
JUJITSU

Jujutsu is a generic term describing a number of combat systems. These originated in the Heian period (AD 794–1185), although the collective title was not applied until much later. Although *jujutsu* was mainly concerned with unarmed versus unarmed or armed opponents, it also dealt, to a lesser extent, with the use of weapons. Included in the repertoire were methods of kicking, striking, throwing, choking and locking of the joints to restrain an opponent.

Historically *jujutsu* served as a kind of insurance against losing one's weapon, the sword. In this sense it was considered a secondary art to swordmanship. The principles of *atemi* – striking the weak points of the opponent – were developed in *jujutsu*, and are still used today in Aikido as a means to break the balance of *uke* or strike him if he does not 'follow' the technique being applied. *Ju* is the name of a Chinese character the meaning of which includes pliable, yielding, adaptable, harmonious, but certainly not weak. In *jujutsu*, defence is achieved by yielding to the attack, but not to the attacker. Thus the basic rules apply: push when pulled; pull when pushed.

Jigoro Kano created judo in 1882. Linguistically it appears to be a *do* form of *jujutsu*; certainly the origins of judo lie in *jujutsu*, and Kano's original intentions were not to emphasise sport or competition. However, judo has long since been seized upon as a competitive sport. There are those who still retain elements of *budo* in their practice of judo, but these few are the exceptions.

Aikido principles also draw heavily on certain aspects of *jujutsu*. For example, the concept of yielding to, or absorbing, the attacker's force, and many of the locks, throws and *atemi*, have a recognizable counterpart in Aikido.

When I first started practising Aikido I heard from one source that Aikido was a twentieth-century creation. Elsewhere I was led to believe that Aikido was an ancient art of the medieval *samurai*. The confusion began to resolve itself when I learned how O Sensei took the knowledge of the past as his 'base metal' and forged it in the furnace of his spirit, to create a new and precious element – Aikido.

GLOSSARY

ai The principle of harmony.

aikido The Way of harmony of *ki.*

aikidoka Student of aikido.

atemi Art of striking vital points.

bo A long staff, approximately 6½ feet long.

bokken Japanese hardwood training sword.

bu Literally martial valour. Originally meant to signify 'prevent two weapons coming together'.

budo Martial Way.

budoka Student of *budo.*

bujutsu Warrior arts.

bushi Warrior.

bushido The Way of the warrior; refers to code of honour.

dan Rank; degrees of black belt.

do Way, as in spiritual path.

dojo Place where the Way is practised, be it martial arts or *zen* meditation.

gi Uniform for the practice of martial arts; usually white.

hakama Divided skirt worn over *gi* in Aikido; usually black or dark blue.

hanmi Stance.

hara Centre, both physical and spiritual; approximately 1 inch below the navel.

iaido The Way of sword drawing, striking and sheathing.

ikkyo The first immobilization in Aikido.

irimi Entering movement.

irimi nage Entering throw.

jo Short staff, approximately 4 feet long.

ju Principle of suppleness.

judo Way of suppleness; popular sporting martial art.

jujutsu Mainly unarmed combat skills based on the supple Way.

kamae Posture.

kami Divine spirit.

kamiza   Small altar at the head of the mat, opposite which sit the students at the start of the class. Usually there is a picture of the Founder and a small offering.

kata   Form; a series of basic movements repeated in sequence.

katana   Japanese sword.

katate tori   One-handed wrist-grab attack.

kendo   Literally the way of the sword; but refers to Japanese fencing.

kenjutsu   The study of sword-fighting techniques.

ki   Energy, physical or spiritual, or of life itself.

koan   *Zen* riddle designed to facilitate *satori.*

kokyu   The power of *ki* extending through the body; relating to the breath.

kokyu nage   Breath throw.

kyu   Rank; below *dan.*

maai   Fighting distance; good *maai* normally requires one entering step to place the attacker at the correct distance to strike a blow.

nage   Person receiving attack, who performs the Aikido technique.

nikyo   Second immobilization.

obi   Belt.

omote   In front; refers to direction of movement of technique.

ryu   School or style of *budo*; usually following blood lines.

samurai   *Bushi* of the Muromachi period.

sankyo   Third immobilization.

satori   Enlightenment.

seiza   A kneeling position.

sensei   Teacher.

shihan   Highest ranking teacher.

shikko   Knee-walking.

Shinto   National religion of Japan.

shomen   Head.

shomen-uchi   Vertical blow to the head.

suwari-waza   Sitting technique.

tachi-waza   Standing technique.

tai-sabaki   Body movement.

takemusu Literally martial creative. Relates to highest level of Aikido; beyond form.

tanden Physical and spiritual centre. See *hara*.

tatami Mat on which *budo* is practised.

tenkan Circular turning movement.

uke Literally receiver (of the technique); attacker in Aikido.

ukemi Art of regaining the balance through falling and rolling.

ura Behind; refers to direction of movement of technique.

waza Technique.

yokomen-uchi Blow to the side of the head.

yonkyo Fourth immobilization.

zazen *Zen* meditation.

zen Meditative school of Buddhism.

JAPANESE NUMERALS

ichi One.

ni Two.

san Three.

shi Four.

go Five.

roku Six.

shichi Seven.

hach Eight.

ku Nine.

jyu Ten.

REFERENCE SECTION

USEFUL ADDRESSES

Aikikai World Headquarters
17-18 Wakamatsu-cho
Shirijuku-Ku
Tokyo 162
Japan
Tel. no. 81-3-3203-9236
Fax. no. 81-3-3204-8145

International Aikido Federation
General Secretary
c/o. Aikido World Headquarters
17-18 Wakamatsu-cho
 Shinijuku-ku, Tokyo 162
Japan

British Aikido Board
General Secretary
6 Halkingcroft
Langley,
Slough SL3 7AT
Tel. 01753 819 086
Fax. 01753 675 816

British Aikido Federation
Peter Megann
Yew Tree Cottage
Toot Baldon
Oxford OX44 9NE
Tel/Fax. 01865 343 500

United Kingdom Aikikai
Allan Roberts
6 Wombrook Dale
Wombourne
Staffs WV5 8HL
Tel. 01902 896 211

Aikido Yoshinkai
Tony Yates
44 Valley Walk
Croxley Green
Watford WD3 3TG
Tel. 01923 218 180

British Aikido Association (Tomiki School)
Martin Thorne
The Ridge
Bridstow
Buckcastle Hill
nr. Ross-on-Wye
HR9 6QF
Tel: 01989 565 517

British Aikido Association (Tomiki)
The Chairman
3-16-9 Kamiikedai
Ota-ku
Tokyo 145
Japan

Kai Shin Kai (Traditional)
Vincent Sumpter
65 Vanner Road
Whitney
Oxon OX8 6LL
Tel. 01993 772 709

The Tomiki School
British
British Aikido Association
V. Sumpter
Secretary
65 Vanner Road
Whitney
Oxfordshire OX8 6LL
tel: 0993 772709
International
R.H. Kogure
Chairman
Japan Aikido Association
3–16–9 Kamiikedai
Ota-ku
Tokyo 145
Japan

BIBLIOGRAPHY

Deshimaru, T. (1982) *The Zen Way to the Martial Arts*, W.P. Dutton, New York.

Draeger, D.F. (1980) *Comprehensive Asian Fighting Arts*, Kodansha International, Tokyo.

Hyams, J. (1979) *Zen in the Martial Arts*, J.P. Archer, Los Angeles.

Klickstein, B. (1987) *Living Aikido*, North Atlantic Books, California.

Lowry, D. (1986) *Bokken – Art of the Japanese Sword*, O'Hara, California.

Makiyama, T.H. (1983) *Keijutsukai Aikido – Japanese Art of Self-Defense*, O'Hara, California.

Reid, H. Croucher M. (1983) *The Way of the Warrior – the Paradox of the Martial Arts*, Century, London.

Saito, M. (1973) *Traditional Aikido – Sword, Stick and Body Arts*, vol. 1, Minato Research and Publishing Co. Tokyo.

Saito, M. (1975) *Aikido – Its Heart and Appearance*, Minato Research and Publishing Co. Tokyo.

Shioda, G. (1968) *Dynamic Aikido*, translated by G. Hamilton, Kodansha International, Tokyo.

Stevens, J. (1985) *Aikido – the Way of Harmony*, Shambala, Boston and London.

Stevens, J. (1987) *Abundant Peace – the Biography of Morihei Ueshiba, Founder of Aikido*, Shambala, Boston and London.

Suzuki, S. (1970) *Zen Mind Beginner's Mind*, Weatherhill, New York and Tokyo.

Tohei, K. (1961) *Aikido – The Arts of Self-Defense*, Rikugei, Tokyo.

Ueshiba, K. (1984) *The Spirit of Aikido*, Kodansha, Tokyo.

Ueshiba, K. (1985) *Aikido*, Hozansha, Tokyo.

Westbrook, A., Ratti, O. (1970) *Aikido and the Dynamic Sphere*, Charles E. Tuttle, Vermont.

Zier, D., Lang T. (1985) *Jo – The Japanese Short Staff*, Unique, California.

INDEX

Page numbers in *italic* refer to the illustrations